In Their
Own Voice

In Their Own Voice

Women and Irish Nationalism

Margaret Ward

ATTIC PRESS
Dublin

First published in Ireland in 1995 by
Attic Press
29 Upper Mount Street
Dublin 2

ISBN 1 85594 101 5

A catalogue record for this book is available from the British Library.

Cover design: Michael O'Dwyer
Cover photo: National Library of Ireland
Typesetting: Jimmy Lundberg Desktop Publishing
Printing: The Guernsey Press Co. Ltd

Attic Press receives financial assistance from the Arts Council/An Comhairle Ealaíon, Ireland.

For Paddy,
Fintan and Medbh

CONTENTS

ACKNOWLEDGEMENTS

'A Servant of the Queen' by Maud Gonne MacBride, reproduced by permission of Colin Smythe Ltd.

The Years Flew By by Sydney Gifford Czira, reproduced by kind permission of Gifford and Craven.

The Howth Gun-Running and *University College Dublin* by F X Martin reproduced by kind permission of the Educational Company of Ireland.

Revolutionary Woman: Kathleen Clarke, edited by Helen Litton, reproduced by permission of the O'Brien Press.

Mother of All the Behans by Brian Behan, reproduced by kind permission of Century Hutchinson UK and Poolbeg Press, Ireland.

Excerpts from *Survivors*, edited by Uinseann Mac Eoin, reproduced by kind permission of the author and Argenta Publications.

Excerpts from the autobiography of Máire Comerford reproduced by kind permission of Joe Comerford.

Hanna Sheehy-Skeffington Papers, reproduced by kind permission of Andrée Sheehy-Skeffington.

Papers from the National Library of Ireland reproduced by kind permission of the Trustees of the National Library.

Excerpts from the Second Dáil debates on the Treaty reproduced by kind permission of the Controller, Stationery Office, Dublin.

Letter to Eva Gore-Booth reproduced by kind permission of Josslyn Gore-Booth.

Every effort has been made to trace the owners of copyright material. Where such efforts have been unsuccessful, any omission will be corrected in future editions if brought to the attention of the publisher.

I am grateful to many people for their help. Michael and Orla Farrell have provided unfailing support in countless ways. The enthusiasm shown by Liz Curtis, as well as her suggestions for material, is greatly appreciated. Thanks to Ailbhe Smyth, inspirer of feminists everywhere, for enabling yet another visit to Dublin to be made. Helen Litton and Medb Ruane know how important their contribution has been. Mike Tomlinson successfully bridged the gap between Bristol and Belfast. Thanks to Brighid Mhic Sheain for material on Alice Milligan. The prompt response to my proposal from Ríona MacNamara and Attic Press was immensely encouraging. The library staff at Bath College of Higher Education coped with a flood of requests, and the assistance of the staff in the National Library of Ireland is gratefully acknowledged. I am also indebted to the support of colleagues in the History Department at Bath College. Most of all, love and gratitude to Paddy, Fintan and Medbh for understanding.

Introduction

THIS collection of documents enables some of the women who took part in the movement for Irish national independence to be heard in their many different voices – expressing their hopes and dreams, their criticisms and their disappointments, their terrors and their refusal to accept defeat. This is their voice, as they wrote in the newspapers of the day and as they explained themselves in autobiographies, letters and speeches. Commentary and interpretation have been kept to a minimum: their words have shaped the ordering of the material, the headings suggesting themselves after the extracts had been gathered. I wanted to reveal voices as they would be found if one were to enter the world of dusty tomes, precious files of manuscripts and the intricacies of microfich and microfilm. It is not easy, finding this voice. Much of it is buried, accessible only to those with the time to explore the archives. Much more of it, I am certain, has still to be found. The archives have not been fully explored, while family sideboards and attics may still yield treasures concerning past relatives, of whom not much was known other than that they were 'involved' in something, many years ago. Local studies have hardly begun and they have the potential to reveal much information on the realities of political life and social relationships in rural Ireland.

This collection focuses upon only one aspect of Irish life: women's contribution to the struggle for national independence and their never-ceasing attempts to gain acceptance as political equals. There are books on other, related, topics, that need to be produced. We need to read about the concerns of the suffrage movement; we need to know what women in the labour movement were saying and doing; and women whose political sympathies were with the Unionist cause also need to have their voice recovered for this generation. Turning away from the obviously political, we also want to know what women from all the different religious, political and social groups thought about those important everyday issues that affect us all – love, marriage, children, health, education, work – only then will we be close to recovering our past and through this, to arriving at some understanding of the complex roots that have made our society what it is today.

My hope is that this book, and others that may be published in the future, will provide an incentive to those who would like to set up a women's studies course, or a women in Irish history course, and are held back because of a lack of sufficient material. For teachers of history, the need for 'primary sources' often determines what courses are developed and what never see the light of day. As more is published on the history of women in Ireland, current explanations and justifications for not teaching students about women will be revealed for what they are – lame excuses. For those who will use this book as a teaching aid, I hope there is enough material to provide hours of fruitful discussion. For those of you who simply want to read it, I hope it proves illuminating. And most of all, I hope that the words spoken and written by that past generation of women will provide some kind of pointer for all those engaged in the process of ensuring that women will be central to the process currently underway in this island – the creation of a democracy which recognises the contribution that all can make to the development of a society of free and equal human beings.

Margaret Ward,
January 1995.

CHAPTER 1

The Nationalist Revival

FINDING A PLACE IN THE MOVEMENT

Maud Gonne was the first woman to be publicly associated with the Irish nationalist cause since the dissolution of the Ladies' Land League in 1882. In 1888, six years after this event, she came to Ireland, a new convert to the cause. As the following extract from her autobiography makes plain, there was nothing she could join. All nationalist organisations excluded women from membership.

Oldham said, I must meet the Fenian leader, John O'Leary, and asked me to a meeting of the Contemporary Club, of which he was secretary, and where O'Leary was generally present. In his original way, Oldham introduces me to the Club in this fashion: 'Maud Gonne wants to meet John O'Leary; I thought you would all like to meet Maud Gonne.'

I glanced round the cosy room, looking over College Green, where some twelve men were sitting smoking and drinking tea, and I felt a little doubtful about the last part of the introduction, for no women were admitted to the Club; it was only later that a monthly ladies' night was arranged.

A tall, thin, strikingly handsome old man rose from an armchair by the fire, with a puzzled frown on his face (I say old, because when one is twenty, anyone over forty appears old – John O'Leary was only in middle age). He came towards me. I felt very shy, but taking my courage in both hands, I said in a low voice: 'Mr O'Leary, I have heard so much about you; you are the leader of revolutionary Ireland, I want to work for Ireland, I want you to show me how.'

John O'Leary liked direct talk; the frown vanished from his eyes, which always reminded me of the eyes of a caged eagle. Instead, an eager look came into them as he led me to a sofa, while Mr Oldham busied himself in supplying me with a cup of tea. I told him my people were all Unionists, that my father was dead and that I had determined to devote my life to working for Ireland, but didn't know how to begin.

O'Leary was very interested. I found that along with his hobby, the collection of rare books, his chief interest in life was getting new

3

recruits for Ireland, especially from the Unionist element from which he wanted to form an intellectual backing for the Separatist movement, and I was a possible new recruit. He soon found out, I expect, that I was not intellectual, but I was young and he was hopeful.

'You must read,' he said, 'read the history of our country, read its literature; I will lend you the books and then you must lecture.'

And we arranged that I should have tea with him and his sister Ellen, next day. Meanwhile the Club debate was beginning. I think it was Dr Sigerson who took the chair; I was invited to remain. They were debating some phase of the Land League, and to my surprise I found that John O'Leary was bitterly opposed to it, especially in its later developments, and was scathingly sarcastic about the Parliamentary leaders and their mock heroics in refusing to wear prison clothes, and also about the so-called 'Union of Hearts.'...

Several gentlemen, whom I took to be professional and business men, hardly said anything; like myself, they sat, listening silently and thoroughly enjoying it. An old farmer from Donegal, on a visit to Dublin, occasionally threw in a trenchant unanswerable remark in favour of the Land League, and though O'Leary disagreed with him, I saw he respected and liked him. Only once I raised my voice, and ventured to ask about the Ladies' Land League, recently suppressed, and was told by John O'Leary: – 'They may not have been right, but they were suppressed because they were honester and more sincere than the men.'...

I was inundated with requests to recite at Workmen's clubs and Literary societies. I recited some of Davis's poems to illustrate a lecture of Willie Rooney's at the Celtic Literary Society, and I met there Arthur Griffith for the first time. He was a fair, shy boy one would hardly notice, but I was at once attracted to him, I hardly knew why, for he did not speak, and I got to know him well only in 1899 when he and Willie Rooney came to me with the first copy of the United Irishman. They had collected £30 and hoped it would be enough to start the paper, and found they had not even enough for the second Number.

The Celtic Literary Society produced a Manuscript Journal, *An Seanachie,* which I found very interesting. I was so delighted with the Club and its activities, that I told the secretary I wanted to become a member. He looked embarrassed. Willie Rooney was called to explain, as politely as he could, that the rules of the Club excluded women from membership.

Laughingly I told the Committee of the Celtic Literary Society that I would have to start a Women's society and I would get all their sisters and sweethearts into it, and they would have to look to their laurels then.

4

Arthur Griffith and Willie Rooney both disapproved of the exclusion of women and, when I did actually start *Inghinidhe na hEireann* in 1900, gave me all the help they could, and the Celtic Literary Society generously lent us their rooms for our meetings and classes, till we were big enough to have a house of our own, and run lectures on History and Irish, dancing, singing and drilling classes for children in three halls in Dublin. Later the Celtic Literary Society admitted women to membership.

I took rooms in the Gresham Hotel, until I could get a flat. Almost opposite to the Gresham Hotel were the offices of the National League. Passing the door, I went in and told the clerk in the outer office I wished to subscribe and become a member. He ushered me into a large room with a great table down the centre and rows of chairs for meetings; it was rather impressive. From the inner office a secretary appeared, a genial young man called Quinn. He at once congratulated me on my recitations and on my letter in the Press against the playing of the English National Anthem at an Irish Concert and said he was sure his Chief, Mr Harrington, – who was out, – would like to meet me, and enquired what time I would be in for him to call. I then told him I wanted to join the National League and was ready to do any work suggested. He also looked embarrassed and said:

'There are no ladies in the National League.'

'How strange,' I replied. 'Surely Ireland needs all her children.'

Decidedly there was no place for women in the National movement.

Next day, Tim Harrington, weather-beaten and very able, a man to count with, called on me. He was accompanied by two other M.P.s whom he introduced. T.P. Gill, pale and lanky, a typical clerk, and Pat O'Brien, small and companionable. I longed to ask Harrington if he had brought them to chaperone him in an interview with a dangerous lady, but didn't dare.

...I told Mr Harrington that at the National League offices I had been informed no women were admitted to membership. Mr Harrington's blue eyes twinkled merrily as he said:

'The Constitution of the National League does not allow lady members.'

'But there used to be a Ladies' Land League and they did splendid work.'

'Indeed they did,' said Pat O'Brien; 'they were great women and kept things lively while we were all in jail.'

'We disbanded the Ladies' Land League when we came out,' said Harrington, I thought a little bitterly. 'They did too good work, and some of us found they could not be controlled.'

'But don't you approve of women in politics, Mr Harrington?'

Again his eyes twinkled and he said, with mock solemnity:

'A woman's place is in the home; but don't be afraid, Miss Gonne, we will find plenty of work for you, if that is what you want.'

I was not satisfied, and said so. 'I know women can do some things better than men, and men can do some things better than we can; but I don't like this exclusion of women from the national fight, and the fact that they should have to work through back-door influence if they want to get things done.'

He looked at me questioningly but kindly. Perhaps he was wondering if I was thinking of a woman who had great influence on his leader Parnell, and who was very much in all their thoughts though her name was rarely mentioned; but I was not – at that time I had never heard of Mrs O'Shea (Stephen Gwynn introduced us later on the Terrace of the House of Commons). He said:

'It is no back-stair work I am going to propose you doing. Have you ever seen evictions?'

I told him I had left a Cavan landlord's house on account of them. 'There have been bad evictions in Donegal and there are going to be more; I suggest you go and see for yourself. You may be able to do publicity work; in any case your presence will hearten the people, and let them see they have strong friends on their side. I will give you a letter of introduction to the Bishop of Raphoe and a list of hotels to stay in; but warn you travelling is rough in those parts. Call in at the League Office. Quinn will have the letters ready for you.'

Maud Gonne MacBride: *A Servant of the Queen*, pp. 89-97.

Mary Macken was one of the first women to succeed in entering higher education. She was awarded a BA in German from the Royal University in 1898, six years after Maud Gonne first attended the Contemporary Club. As her experience shows, during the succeeding decade only slight progress had been made in securing women's admittance to the various discussion groups.

It was not at the Literary Society but at the Contemporary Club that I first had the thrill of meeting Yeats and hearing him talk in what was an intimate circle. I was not a member of the Club – my sex debarred me – but the 'exclusive' males were good enough to admit us to a symposium every fourth Saturday and I, for one, went gladly...

Others who frequented the Club, though they do not all seem to have been members, were Dr Bob Kenny, the Parnellite, T.W. Russell (first as Unionist, then as Minister in the Liberal Government), AE, Sheehy-Skeffington and Padraic Colum. On Ladies' Night I remember well Miss Sara Purser, whose wit was the salt to our meat; Ella Young, a fascinating speaker with a beautiful voice, who wrote verses in the manner of AE – she was one of his 'mystic school'; Alice Oldham, a quiet, effective speaker, deeply intellectual – she was Lecturer in Mental and Moral Science at Alexandra College. The most romantic woman of the age I never met at the Club: Maud Gonne was out of Ireland when my acquaintance with the Contemporary began in 1903. But her miniature hung on the wall, and I heard much of the spell which her beauty and her personality had woven round the work and the life of Yeats. The part of the Countess Cathleen had been written for her; she had 'with weird power' played the title role in Cathleen ni Houlihan at its premiere in 1902, whilst a sonnet – of Shakespeare perhaps and of Ronsard – reforged in Celtic fires, fused the Dark Lady and Helene so that they suffered rich transformation in a Yeats lyric.

Professor Mary Macken, MA: 'Yeats, O'Leary
and the Contemporary Club', in *Studies (Ireland)*, 1939,
pp.137; 139.

ULSTER WOMEN

Alice Milligan was born near Omagh, to a wealthy northern Protestant family. She was a poet and playwright, and for a number of years was organiser for the Gaelic League. In the following extract she describes a scene from her childhood when tales of her old nurse scared the child into fears that the 'Fenians' (or the Catholics) would attack. And as she makes plain, her sympathies as a grown woman were firmly with the radical republican tradition that united all creeds in the fight for independence.

My old nurse related a more detailed reminiscence of the Fenian days. There was one particular night in March, when the rising was anticipated, and no one in the house she was then employed in thought of going to bed. The whole family adjourned to a top room of the house, in the ceiling of which there was a trap door leading to a loft. A ladder was placed against this, and the ladies divested themselves of their crinolines, so as to be able in case of necessity to squeeze through the opening. It was arranged, moreover, that nurse, who was of rotund proportions, was to be last to ascend, as it was doubted whether she would be able to get through the aperture. Towards morning it seems to have been a still, clear night, A whistle was heard going round the house and with a horrified cry of 'Here they come, that's the signal,' there was a rush for the ladder. However, it turned out that this was a bird, a Peeweet, and no Fenian put in an appearance. There were other anxious nights, but gradually the dread diminished, but never quite vanished. All through my own childhood, a sudden noise or outcry in the night set my heart beating and I would start up thinking that the hour had come.

Not long ago I was left alone in a drawing room with a small boy, who after a few minutes of silent meditation, suddenly asked with awe in his voice and fear in his eyes: 'I say, Auntie; do you think there's any chance of the Catholics rising up again?'

To begin with I must explain that this small boy is no relation of mine whatever, and being born in Co. Down, not remote from Saintfield and Ballynahinch, with Presbyterian ancestors, I would have expected him to have inherited a different tradition from the old Protestant massacre terror which I was reared on in Co. Tyrone. I weighed his question considerately. 'Of course, they might rise up some time or other, but there are very few of them in Bangor.' His countenance cleared. 'There aren't enough Catholics in Bangor to rise to do anything. Nearly all the people here are Presbyterians, three Churches full of them.' The last shadow of dread vanished, as he cheerfully thought of the great Presbyterian congregations flocking through the town on Sunday. 'The Catholics here,' I proceeded, 'couldn't manage to do much except the Presbyterians helped them the way they did before.' His eyes became round with bewilderment. 'Sure Presbyterians wouldn't help the Catholics?' 'Oh, yes, dear,' I said. 'In your great-grandfather's time they fought several battles together, and Presbyterian ministers were hanged for it – one at Newtownards and one in Grey Abbey, and several in Belfast were sent to gaol.'

Our conversation was here interrupted by the entrance of a mother and a tea-tray and the youngster was sent off to bed a little eased, I could see, of any haunting dread of having his throat cut by Papists in the dead of night, and much astounded by the newly suggested visions of respectable Presbyterian ministers fighting in Irish rebellions and dangling at rope ends.

Alice Milligan, *The Leader*, 17 July 1909.

THE *SHAN VAN VOCHT*

The Shan Van Vocht was the phonetic version of the Gaelic for 'the poor old woman', a symbolic representation of Ireland. It was the name chosen by Alice Milligan and Anna Johnston for the paper they published in Belfast between the years 1896-1899. As a republican journal it was ahead of its time. It published the early writings of James Connolly and it gave great support to Maud Gonne and other women nationalists. In 1898 Irish Nationalists celebrated the centenary of the United Irishmen's Rising of 1798. Much of the preparations for these events were marred by internal dissensions between pro-and anti-Parnellites and also between parliamentarians and those who supported the physical force tradition of the Fenians. The following editorial in the Shan Van Vocht *makes reference to these tensions as it calls for Irish women to come forward and do their bit for the commemoration.*

It is not too much to hope that in the present crisis of our country's history, occasion demands, when, alas! political dissensions are rife, that the women of Ireland, who are not called upon to have any opinion whatever as to who has the right to speak for Ireland in the British Parliament, should form that Union which a historic occasion demands ... We say nothing for or against this policy, but the '98 Commemoration must be kept clear of party. We call upon the women of Ireland to support the organisation now in the course of formation.

Shan Van Vocht, June 1897.

IRISH WOMEN'S CENTENARY UNION

By the end of the summer of 1897 that plea had been acted upon by a number of women in the north of Ireland, as Alice Milligan took pleasure in announcing. An Irish Women's Centenary Union was formed.

For our part we have found a secure and neutral ground in the Irishwomen's Centenary Union, the Committee of which is in course of foundation. Is it not a fortunate thing that the better half (numerically, of course, I mean) of the population of Ireland is not involved in these differences of the polling booths?

In Belfast, when political dissensions have been embittered by an additional and purely local division, it is surely a hopeful and healing sign to see a number of Irishwomen working together on a high and patriotic platform above strife and turmoil. Mrs John Martin, sister of the most honoured patriot that Ulster has produced since '98, is giving active help in forming the committee and has secured for it the addition of the name of one of John Mitchel's daughters, who, though separated from us by the ocean, will be a strong sympathiser. Mrs Martin, though she has strong political opinions, and does not hesitate to declare them, has always acted on the principle that political differences should never interfere in personal friendships, and in this she has shown an example which all Irishwomen would do well to follow. To them is entrusted the moulding of the minds of the growing generations of the Irish race, and they should exercise their influence, so that old quarrels would pass away with the makers of them, and so that those who are to work for Ireland in the new era should be able to do so untrammelled by old feuds and hatreds.

It may be urged that to form a committee solely of women is narrow, but in our opinion, as far, at any rate, as Ulster is concerned, you will best revive interest in the cause of Ireland by some such union amongst women for the purpose. Our aim will be not to exclude men from our sphere of national work, but to revive their interest in it, and to give them safe guidance out of the hurly-burly of the political faction fight into which they have wandered from the straight path. In the North especially many women will be found willing to join in the '98 celebrations whose husbands, or other male relatives, for business reasons, could not possibly do so. Then there is another thing to be looked to. The Government may find it expedient or necessary to forbid some of the demonstrations which the men's committees will organise. No power of law exists to prevent the celebration of '98 in the form which the department under women's management is to be arranged. For the benefit of the pilgrims visiting Ireland next year, we shall aim at getting together and exhibiting relics and portraits of the United men, and for the benefit of the peasantry throughout the country we will organise at suitable centres sales of Irish industries. The care of the neglected and uninscribed graves will be another part of the work, and in Belfast a beginning will be made by placing a tablet with epitaph on the grave of Mary McCracken, at Clifton Street Cemetery.

Shan Van Vocht, September 1897.

THE FAMINE QUEEN

The elderly Queen Victoria visited Ireland in 1900. Her aim was to boost recruitment into the British army, which needed more soldiers to take part in the fight against the Boers in the Transvaal. Maud Gonne's famous polemic against Queen Victoria – the 'Famine Queen' – was first printed in her Paris-based paper L'Irelande Libre. *When it was reprinted in the* United Irishman, *the authorities suppressed the paper to prevent people from reading it.*

'The Queen's visit to Ireland is in no way political,' proclaims the Lord Lieutenant, and the English ministers. 'The Queen's visit has no political signification, and the Irish nation must receive her Majesty with the generous hospitality for which it is celebrated,' hastens to repeat Mr John Redmond, and our servile Irish members whose nationality has been corrupted by a too lengthy sojourn in the enemy's country.

'The Queen's visit to Ireland has nothing at all to do with politics,' cries the fishmonger, Pile, whose ambitious soul is not satisfied by the position of Lord Mayor and who hankers after an English title. 'Let us to our knees, and present the keys of the city to her Most Gracious Majesty, and compose an address in her honour.'

'Nothing political! nothing political! let us present an address to this virtuous lady,' echo 30 town councillors, who when they sought the votes of the Dublin people called themselves Irishmen and Nationalists, but who are overcome by royal glamour. Poor citizens of Dublin! your thoughtlessness in giving your votes to these miserable creatures will cost you dear. It has already cost the arrests of sixteen good and true men, and many broken heads and bruised limbs from police batons, for you have realised – if somewhat late – the responsibility of Ireland's capital, and, aghast at the sight of the men elected by you betraying and dishonouring Ireland, you have, with a courage which makes us all proud of you, raised a protest, and cried aloud, 'The visit of the Queen of England is a political action, and if we accord her a welcome we shall stand shamed before the nations. The world will no longer believe in the sincerity of our demand for National Freedom!'

And in truth, for Victoria, in the decrepitude of her eighty-one years, to have decided after an absence of half-a-century to revisit the country she hates and whose inhabitants are the victims of the criminal policy of her reign, the survivors of sixty years of organised famine, the political necessity must have been terribly strong; for after all she is a woman, and however vile and selfish and pitiless her soul may be, she must sometimes tremble as death approaches when she thinks of the countless Irish mothers who, shelterless under the cloudy Irish sky, watching their starving little ones, have cursed her before they died.

Every eviction during sixty-three years has been carried out in Victoria's name, and if there is a Justice in Heaven the shame of those poor Irish emigrant girls whose very innocence renders them an easy prey and who have been overcome in the terrible struggle for existence on a foreign shore, will fall on this woman, whose bourgeoise virtue is so boasted and in whose name their homes were destroyed. If she comes to Ireland again before her death to contemplate the ruin she has made it is surely because her ministers and advisors think that England's situation is dangerous and that her journey will have a deep political importance. England has lived for years on a prestige which has had no solid foundation. She has hypnotised the world with the falsehood of her greatness; she has made great nations and small nations alike, believe in her power. It required the dauntless courage and energy of the Boers to destroy for ever this illusion and rescue Europe from the fatal enchantment. To-day no one fears the British Empire, her prestige has gone down before the rifles of a few thousand heroic peasants.

If the British Empire means to exist she will have to rely on real strength, and real strength she has not got. England is in decadence. She has sacrificed all to getting money, and money cannot create men, nor give courage to her weakly soldiers. The men who formerly made her greatness, the men from the country districts have disappeared; they have been swallowed up by the great black manufacturing cities; they have been flung into the crucible where gold is made. To-day the giants of England are the giants of finance and of the Stock Exchange, who have risen to power on the backs of a struggling mass of pale, exhausted slaves.The storm approaches; the gold which the English have made out of the blood and tears of millions of human beings attracts the covetousness of the world. Who will aid the pirates to keep their spoils? In their terror they turn to Victoria, their Queen. She has succeeded in amassing more gold than any of her subjects; she has always been ready to cover with her royal mantle the crimes and turpitude of her Empire, and now, trembling on the brink of the grave, she rises once more at their call. Soldiers are needed to protect the vampires. The Queen issues an appeal in England, the struggling mass of slaves cry 'Hurrah'; but there is no blood in their veins, no strength in their arms. Soldiers must be found, so Victoria will go herself to fetch them; she will go over to Ireland – to this people who have despised gold, and who, in spite of persecutions and threats, have persisted in their dream of Freedom and idealism, and who, though reduced in numbers, have maintained all the beauty and strength and vitality of their race.

Taking the Shamrock in her withered hand she dares to ask Ireland for soldiers – for soldiers to protect the exterminators of their race! And the reply of Ireland comes sadly but proudly, not through the lips of the miserable little politicans who are touched by the English canker but through the lips of the Irish people:

'Queen, return to your own land; you will find no more Irishmen ready to wear the red shame of your livery. In the past they have done so from ignorance, and because it is hard to die of hunger when one is young and strong and the sun shines, but they shall do so no longer; see! your recruiting agents return unsuccessful and alone from my green hills and plains, because once more hope has revived, and it will be in the ranks of your enemies that my children will find employment and honour! As to those who to-day enter your service to help in your criminal wars, I deny them! If they die, if they live, it matters not to me, they are no longer Irishmen.'

Maud Gonne, *United Irishman*, 7 April 1900.

THE NAMING OF 'SINN FEIN'

A young woman, Máire de Bhuitleir (Mary Ellen Butler), suggested the name 'Sinn Féin' for a new organisation of nationalists that was being planned at the end of 1904. Arthur Griffith said: 'Her name will be ever linked with its history.' Máire de Bhuitleir died suddenly in 1921, not long after writing this account of her memories of those times.

As I write these lines, there lies before me a crumpled little linen badge bearing the words 'SINN FEIN, 1905'. Here is a relic indeed – one to be viewed by the Irish woman with much the same sentiment that might grip her as she surveyed a lock of bright hair from the brow of an infant who, in later years, became a looming giant in the nation's affairs...

When I look on the little linen badge that lies before me, I remember I wore it for the first time as a delegate to the first Convention of the National Council of Sinn Féin, on Tuesday November 28th, 1905. And this is the scene that rises before me: A shabby room in the old Rotunda of Dublin, with less than a hundred men and a handful of women and girls seated in rapt attention.

They are listening to an earnest young man who faces them with a sheaf of papers in his hand. He is very tranquil, very modest, quite unaggressive – yet also full of suppressed flame and ardour. Some of us present do not even know the speaker's name; and presently I catch 'Arthur Griffith' passing from mouth to mouth with eager zeal. I am glad to know that I, at least, was not unaware of the new apostle's identity, nor of his revolutionary evangel. Had I not often called upon him in that untidy den at 6, Harcourt Street? And had I not also dropped in again and again at Arthur Griffith's still earlier office at 17, Fownes Street, to converse of things which were near and dear to his great heart? And was it not I – I say it with a thrill of pride – who first proposed to him the title of SINN FEIN for his new vision of self-help among the Irish people?

'No tactics,' Griffith used to say, 'will prevent us from winning the 'ear of Ireland, and holloing into it, as Louis Kossuth did in the ear of Hungary. By ourselves and on our own soil must our national salvation be worked out.'

I shall be asked: From what source did you derive this title? It is hard to say, so vague and uncertain are the tricks of memory. But the early motto of the Gaelic League was: '*Sinn féin, sinn féin, amhain*' – (Ourselves, ourselves alone). Surely no need of faith and hope ever equalled that of Griffith, in the face of overwhelming obstacles and disappointments...

That day in Fownes Street, when once more Arthur Griffith expounded to my sister and me his doctrine of self-sufficiency, passive resistance and abstention from the British Parliament, and so on, I suddenly remarked: 'The policy of Sinn Féin, in fact!'

And Griffith pounced upon the saying with delight. 'Sinn Féin,' he cried, 'are exactly the two words which express my meaning.'

> Máire de Bhuitleir: 'When the Sinn Féin Policy Was Launched' in (ed.) W G Fitzgerald: *The Voice of Ireland*, pp. 105-9

THE DOORS OPEN

Jenny Wyse-Power, as young Jenny O'Toole, was a member of the Ladies' Land League. She later became a vice-president of Sinn Féin and ended her public life in 1936 as a Senator in the Free State. Here she pays tribute to the Gaelic League (which from its inception in 1893 included women amongst its members), and to the pioneering work of the early Sinn Féin movement:

Between this period and the birth of the Gaelic League and Sinn Féin, there is nothing to record of the activities of Irishwomen except their attitude during the Parnell crisis. It was then seen that if our women had the vote, the bye-elections fought would have had very different results.

The echoes of the Parnell affair had not yet died when a new movement was inaugurated by the founding of the Gaelic League. This novel cultural body rejected the false sex and class distinctions which were the result of English influence. And to the Gaelic League is due the credit of having established the first Irish national society which accepted women as members on the same terms as men.

From the beginning, women sat on its Branch Committees and Executive, and helped to carry out the programme. The work was of such a nature that women's help was essential. The study of the Irish language was for all; the social side was almost wholly in the hands of the women members, who by absorbing the Irish tradition, and themselves giving expression to Gaelic ideals and culture, influenced in no small degree the growing effort to wean the people from an

Anglicisation which had gone all too far.

In 1905 the Sinn Féin movement was formally launched at a public meeting in the Dublin Rotunda. Its growth was slow, for its policy of abstention from Westminster seemed at first too novel to a people whose eyes had been so long turned to the 'Mother of Parliaments.' But the seeds of the subsequent revolution were carefully sown in those years by the late Arthur Griffith; and it is noteworthy that throughout the sowing period of many years, and during the recent years of reaping, the Executive of this powerful organisation has never been without a woman member.

We were asked to support Irish manufacturers, and here women naturally played a prominent part, both in private and public, many of them being now members of the elected Boards throughout the country. Women speakers began to be heard at public meetings; and from now on it may be safely stated that their influence was completely on the side of Irish Ireland, which was to say an Ireland wholly separated from England.

In their capacity as Poor Law Guardians, women used their influence to break down the English Poor Law system, under which Irish money was misspent and the Irish poor completely demoralised. Looking back on those years, it is pleasant to recall that our efforts in this direction have materialised, for the Poor Law as then administered has now ceased to exist. No longer are the sick and the strong, the decent and the criminal classes herded together, as under English rule; and throughout Ireland (except in a few places where local difficulties stand in the way) the pernicious Elizabethan Poor Law system is for ever at an end.

Senator Mrs J. Wyse-Power:
'The Political Influence of Women in Modern Ireland'
in (ed.) W G Fitzgerald: *The Voice of Ireland*, pp. 158-61

CHAPTER 2

Inghinidhe na h-Éireann

THE FIRST MEETING

Inghinidhe na h-Éireann (Daughters of Erin) was formed in 1900. For Maud Gonne, its president, it meant an end to working as a 'freelance' for the nationalist cause. A light-hearted account of the formation of the group was printed in their journal, Bean na h-Éireann, *written by 'Maire' – probably Maire Quinn, secretary of the group. The impetus for that first meeting was a desire to present Arthur Griffith with a blackthorn stick in appreciation of his breaking his own stick over the editor of the society paper* Figaro, *which had stated that Maud Gonne was in the pay of the British Government. Griffith had been sent to jail for his action.*

There was in Dublin in 1900 an editor who ran a weekly paper – they passed into oblivion long ago. The paper was then dying; the editor hit upon the expedient of slandering a woman. This, being an unusual hit in a paper published in Ireland, succeeded for that week. Next week there was no editor: he was very, very sore around the back, and head, and hurt in mind because he had been thrashed by a man. This man was an editor also. He got a fortnight 'hard' for giving that thrashing. The papers also reported that his stick or whip was broken.

Now, there were some young girls in Dublin, chiefly members of the Irish classes of the Celtic Literary Society. They knew the man and felt sorry that he had lost his stick. They resolved to replace it. They borrowed the key of the rooms at 32 Lower Abbey Street from a friendly Celtic member and held a meeting on Easter Sunday after 12 Mass. They subscribed the price of a nice, strong blackthorn with a silver ring, bearing an Irish inscription, and decided to present it when the man came out of jail. There were about fifteen girls present, and they discussed other things too. But I must finish talking about the stick and the man. He did not like presentations. And he did not like talking to girls. That was because he did not know them. He has greatly improved. When he came out of jail he was conducted to the Celtic Literary Society Rooms. In the hall it was broken gently to him what was on foot upstairs. He offered to go back to jail another month sooner than face it. He could not, however, the hall door even was

17

locked. He asked a deputation to explain to the girls that it was a printer's error to state that his whip was broken. It was an unbreakable *sjam-bok* he used. The girls did not want any explanation. And the man came along. There was a rumour that he said he wished it had been some of the others who had smashed up the editor. But this is not authenticated, and I do not believe it. But though he received the stick bravely he has not used it much on editors. I wonder why?

Those girls did more than talk about the man, the stick and the editor. They discussed the best way for dressing the hair (I have to tell it, because *Bean na h-Éireann* said that all I remember is to be recorded), and the latest fashions, black and karkhi [sic], because it was the year of the Boer War. And then we spoke of Queen Victoria's visit to Ireland. One said it was a fine idea, that in the 'United Irishman' of that week, of giving a treat to children who refused to go to the park and kow-tow to her majesty, and then the girls all looked at each other and said 'Let us do it.' They were (with one exception) all working girls. They had not much silver and gold to give to Ireland. Only willing hearts, earnestness and determination. All were free on Easter Monday and expressed their readiness to give up the projected pleasure parties in order to go round and collect subscriptions. Then and there the city was mapped into districts, lists of likely subscribers written out and two girls appointed for each district. The girls talked too, of founding a society, and decided on the name 'Inghinidhe na h-Éireann'. The spelling of 'Inghinidhe' was antiquated. That afterwards proved an advertisement for – but of the 'afterwards' – oh, that fine rousing stirring living afterwards, I am not to speak. It will be told you later on by one more competent to deal with it. But you will agree that it was a good morning's work, the presentation of that stick, the undertaking of a patriotic children's treat (there were 30,000 of them) on nothing, and the founding of a women's national society for the advancement of Irish language, literature, history and industries specially amongst the young. What else might have been undertaken no one knows, because the rain came, and the Celtic members cut short their usual Sunday walk, and came in to play chess.

This is the whole history of what took place at the first meeting of the Inghinidhe na h-Éireann.

NB – Except that we decided we would not wear our hair puffed over our ears after the English fashion.

Maire: *Bean na h-Éireann*, May 1910

THE OBJECTS OF INGHINIDHE NA h-ÉIREANN

The re-establishment of the complete independence of Ireland.

To encourage the study of Gaelic, of Irish literature, History, Music and Art, especially among the young, by the organising and teaching of classes for the above objects.

To support and popularise Irish manufacture.

To discourage the reading and circulation of low English litera-ture, the singing of English songs, the attending of vulgar English entertainments at the theatres and music hall, and to combat in every way English influence, which is doing so much injury to the artistic taste and refinement of the Irish people.

To form a fund called the National Purposes Fund, for the further-ance of the above objects.

United Irishman, 13 October 1900

TEACHING THE YOUNG

The Inghinidhe were very serious in their commitment to spread Irish culture amongst the young. They went to child-ren in the poorest parts of Dublin and taught them the language, music and dancing. All this was done with very little resources, but they had some gifted and enthusiastic teachers. Ella Young, poet and mystic, taught Irish history to the children.

The Daughters of Ireland come new to the art of play-acting; indeed they come new to the Gaelic, to the sagas, and to everything! It does not hamper their enthusiasm – on the contrary it affords them occa-sion for a fiery and untrammelled assault on things as they are. The Society is composed of girls who work hard all day in shops and offices owned for the most part by pro-British masters who may at any moment discharge them for 'treasonable activities'. To be dis-missed in such wise means the semi-starvation of long-continued unemployment. These girls dare it, and subscribe, from not too abundant wages, generous amounts for the hire of halls to be used as class-rooms and for theatre rehearsals. I have undertaken, under their auspices, to teach Irish history by a re-telling of the sagas and hero-tales.

In a room perched at the head of a rickety staircase and overlook-ing a narrow street, I have about eighty denizens of untamed Dublin: newsboys, children who have played in street alleys all their lives, young patriot girls and boys who can scarcely write their own names. Outside there is a continuous din of street cries and rumbling carts. It is almost impossible to shout against it if the windows are open, and more impossible to speak in the smother of dust if the windows are shut. Everyone is standing, closely packed – no room for chairs! They stand there, in ages ranging from nine years to eighteen, ready to listen, if there is anything worth listening to, ready to boo or come to fisticuffs the moment that they are not interested. But they are interested. I do not need to say to anyone, 'These are your heroes!' They have relinquished the luxury of a devil-may-care idleness, and whatever adventures may wait round a street corner, to live in heart and mind with Ireland of long ago: to adventure with Fionn, defend the Ford with Cu-Cullion, and crack jokes with Conan the Bald. Eager-eyed, drawing in breaths of rapturous admiration, their thin hardship-sculptured faces flushed with wrath and pride, they stand there adding new names to the hero-names that they have cherished ever since they could put names together: Cu-Cullion, to Parnell; Brown Diarmid, to Robert Emmet; Fionn, the hero-avenger, to Wolfe Tone.

As they tumble down the narrow stairway, homeward bound, I hear shouts of: 'I'm Cu-Cullion!' 'You're not – I took it first!' 'Fionn was a bigger man!'

'It's Diarmid that's my choice!' 'I'll fight you on it!'

In other rooms the Daughters of Ireland have classes for Irish dancing, Gaelic songs, and the Gaelic language. Since we are reviving everything at once, we pay attention to the ancient Festivals. There are four which divide the year into periods of three months: the Festival of Brigit, the Pure Perpetual Ashless Flame, in February; the Festival of Beltane, the coming of the young Gods who succour the Earth, in May; the Marriage-Festival of Lugh, the Sun, who weds the Sovereignty of Erin in August; the Festival of Samhain, that opens the Inner World, in November. W.B. Yeats was eager to revive these Festivals, and at one time planned with Maud Gonne pageants and dances, but the scheme fell through. The Daughters of Ireland, in honour of these Festivals, put on short plays: acting in them eagerly and dauntlessly as soon as they have memorized the words – and sometimes before! Alice Milligan's play, *The Escape of Red Hugh*, is a prime favourite. The young prince, kidnapped by the English and treacherously imprisoned, is looked upon as a symbol of Ireland: and the cheers that greet his prison-break are not all for the hopes that blossomed once and died with him.

Ella Young: *Flowering Dusk*, pp.70-2

Evidence of the hard work of Inghinidhe members is also given by Maud Gonne, who stressed the political goals of the organisation. Her account accompanied the memoirs of Sydney Gifford who, as 'John Brennan', was a member of the group.

Inghinidhe found an empty loft in Strand Street and in this strange class room, which had to be reached by climbing a ladder into the loft, Maire Perolz taught history and Gaelic by the light of a lantern. 'What matter', she said light-heartedly, 'it only makes it all the more fun.'

Sometimes, for want of music, dancing teachers had to lilt an accompaniment for their pupils. Yet after the first year, pupils had won first and second prizes at the Leinster Feis. We had a children's choir also and by the second year started a hurling club for boys. One member was Sean Connolly, who was also in the dramatic class.

Inghinidhe never lost sight of the fact that the objects of the society were not merely cultural and educational, but to work for the complete independence of Ireland; so all children attending our classes were pledged never to enlist in the British Army or Navy. Before the end of the first year we had started a fund for organising National Boys Brigades to prevent enlistment and received a generous subscription from the Ladies' Auxiliary of the Ancient Order of Hibernians American Alliance, Suffolk County, USA. The plan did not come to fruition until nine years later when Con Markievicz of Inghinidhe organised Fianna Eireann.

Every year there was held a great xmas treat for children attending classes as well as taking them to places of historic interest during the summer months. The first at a workman's club had 1,200 children so we had to arrange two entertainments as the club wouldn't hold that number. There were magic lantern displays of the Boer War, the Famine, Irish history as well as a ceili and feast.

To raise funds for the classes we gave a series of entertainments – *tableaux vivants* – and after two years these girls, who were working for their living during the day and teaching our classes on most nights of the week, had formed a dramatic class, so that they could perform plays to raise funds for the work to which they were devoted. Molly and Sara Allgood and some of the other girls suggested the idea of the dramatic class ... The class was taught by me when I was in Dublin and by Dudley Digges in my absence.

Maud Gonne: *Czira Papers* ms 18,817, National Library of Ireland

ADDRESS TO THE WOMEN ELECTORS
OF THE CITY OF DUBLIN
BY INGHINIDHE NA h-Éireann

Hearing that Victoria's successor, Edward VII, was due in Dublin, nationalists organised to deny him the kind of civic welcome given to his mother. Inghinidhe women were prominent in this. Dublin

Corporation was prevented from presenting the royal couple with a loyal address of welcome – a victory which turned out to be an important landmark in encouraging people to believe that nationalists were capable of mobilising an effective opposition.

Fellow country-women – being a purely national society, whose chief object is to cultivate the spirit of ardent patriotism and devotion to Ireland among the young, Inghinidhe na hEireann does not take part in Municipal politics except when some grave National issue, which interests alike men and women, is involved. Such today is the case. It is announced that the English King is coming to Ireland on April 14th. There are many reasons why the Irish people should not welcome Edward VII. As Catholics, remembering the Oath he swore at his Coronation, they should not do so. As decent men and women, they should not do so. Above all, as Irishmen and women, they should not do so. England is the country which is oppressing and ruining Ireland. It is therefore a matter of serious national importance that the cowards or traitors who, pretending to be Nationalists, disgraced Ireland's Capital by welcoming Victoria or by staying away from the Council Chamber allowed the address of welcome to be voted, should be turned out of the Corporation. The following are the gentlemen who betrayed the nationalists of Dublin on the occasion of Victoria's visit two years ago, and whom you have now an opportunity of voting against ...

> Maud Gonne - President
> Máire T. Quinn - Hon. Sec.

United Irishman, 11 January 1902

KATHLEEN NÍ HOULIHAN
Members of Inghinidhe na h-Éireann, together with men from the Celtic Literary Society, were involved in encouraging the establishment of a native Irish dramatic movement. Alice Milligan and Padraic Colum were two writers who contributed their first plays to the group. In 1902 the most ambitious project of the Irish National Dramatic Company was the staging of two new plays: AE's Deirdre *and W.B. Yeats's* Kathleen Ní Houlihan.

We rehearsed when – and where – we could. The performance was scheduled for the hall of St Teresa's Temperance Society in Clarendon Street but it was not until a week before we opened that we had the use of the stage. Sometimes we went out to AE's house at Rathgar to try out *Deirdre*. On other occasions we descended on the homes of sympathetic friends and took possession of libraries and drawing-rooms – anywhere that did not too obviously upset the occupants. Alternatively, of course, if Fay was what he called 'flush', or between us we could muster the necessary cash, we took the Coffee-palace where we fitted as much as we could into a few valuable hours. In the meantime Fay and AE painted scenery...

St Teresa's Hall, Clarendon Street, Dublin, where *Deirdre* and *Kathleen Ní Houlihan* were produced on April 2nd, 3rd, and 4th, 1902, was approached from the Dublin South City markets, off Exchequer Street. It was a small place, with a capacity of about three hundred, and had a little stage which did not give much room for movement or extravagant gesture. The boxed-in scene, manufactured by Willie Fay, took up most of the space from wall to wall. Off-stage during the action, we lined up in the wings in the order of our appearance, backs to the wall, noses almost touching the side-pieces of the scene, and sidled crab-like into position for our entrances. Awaiting our cues, we held our breath. It was quite likely that a vigorous movement would have brought our chests into contact with the canvas walls and caused them to fall inwards. As it was, the whole scene wobbled dangerously when we moved.

There were no dressing-rooms. We had to dress upstairs and get back-stage through the auditorium before the audience began to arrive. This meant that if there were any late-comers amongst the cast they would have to show themselves to the audience before the curtain went up. Maud Gonne arrived late the first night and caused a minor sensation by sweeping though the auditorium in the ghostly robes of the Old Woman in *Kathleen Ní Houlihan* ten minutes before we were due to begin. Frank Fay pursed his lips and stamped away in annoyance from his peep-hole in the proscenium when he saw the occurrence. 'Unprofessional!' he called it ...

Long before the curtain rose, the hall was filled with a mixed gathering of the Ormond Dramatic Society clientele, and a representative cross-section of the literary and artistic cliques of the period. Gleaming shirt-fronts mingled with the less resplendent garb of the Dublin worker, in the tiny auditorium. Before the footlights lit up the banner of Inghinidhe na hEireann – a golden sunburst on a blue ground – hanging near the stage, the aisles were crowded with standing patrons. It was an auspicious opening.

How many who were there that night will forget the Kathleen Ní Houlihan of Maud Gonne, her rich golden hair, willow-like figure, pale sensitive face, and burning eyes, as she spoke the closing lines of the Old Woman turning out through the cottage door:

> 'They shall be remembered forever,
> They shall be alive forever,
> They shall be speaking forever,
> The people shall hear them forever...!'

Watching her, one could readily understand the reputation she enjoyed as the most beautiful woman in Ireland, the inspiration of the whole revolutionary movement. She was the most exquisitely-fashioned creature I have ever seen. Her beauty was startling. Yeats wrote *Kathleen Ní Houlihan* specially for her, and there were few in the audience who did not see why. In her, the youth of the country saw all that was magnificent in Ireland. She was the very personification of the figure she portrayed on the stage.

Maire Nic Shiubhlaigh: *The Splendid Years*, pp. 14, 16-19

BEAN NA h-Éireann
In 1908 the Inghinidhe launched Bean na h-Éireann. *It was edited by Helena Moloney, the first nationalist-feminist journal to be produced in Ireland. Sydney Gifford described the experience of working for it.*

The Inghinidhe had now decided to launch on a new venture – a patriotic monthly magazine for Irishwomen, and I had been asked to a committee meeting to discuss this   proposal.

I had heard a lot about the Inghinidhe na h-Éireann before that night when I first met some of them at their house in North Great George's Street. They were going along O'Connell Street every night distributing handbills into the hands of Irish girls who were walking out with British soldiers, appealing to them not to associate with the 'enemies of their country'.

In Dublin in those days O'Connell Street was divided into two zones, the west side being given over to the British military and their girls, and the east to Dublin civilians. Invading the British zone, the Inghinidhe began distributing their handbills. Needless to say, they were often mobbed by infuriated soldiers and their girls, and had to run to sanctuary on the civilian side of the street, where they were always sure of finding supporters.

As I walked into the committee room, feeling rather overawed, I had a romantic picture in my mind of what these women would look like. They would be just like the heroines of '98 which I had often seen on the supplements to the *Freeman's Journal* I was sure. There was nothing dramatic, however, in the sight that met my eyes in that room. A few women were sitting round a table, earnestly discussing the plans for launching the paper. They were all plainly dressed in costumes of Donegal tweed in shades of dingy browns or greys, which were the chief or only colours in which it was manufactured in those days. But I soon learned that Donegal tweed was just the dust cover on the Movement.

There was a living, breathing romance inside, peopled with real heroes and heroines. I found inside these dust covers those who afterwards became my lifelong friends.

Soon after the meeting started there was a dramatic interlude. The door opened, and a radiant creature burst quickly into the room. She was a tall, beautiful woman, with classical features and a delicate complexion. A diamond ornament glittered in her soft, wavy brown hair, which was dressed in the Grecian style. She had grey eyes, fringed with long, dark lashes. She was wearing a lovely ballgown of blue velvet with the fashionable train of the period. It was a pouring wet night, and the rain was running down into her shoes from the fur cloak thrown round her shoulders.

'Good evening. So sorry for being late – must take off my wet shoes', said Madame Markievicz, all in one breath; and walking over to the fire she took off her two shoes, placing one on each hob. Then without a moment's pause she joined in the discussion round the table.

Before she left that night she had offered to sell the diamond ornament she was wearing to raise funds for the paper. The committee refused to accept her offer, but I feel sure that she sacrificed it later on for some other scheme connected with the Movement.

We walked to the tram together and I noticed that she had forgotten to lift her train, and it dragged in the mud. 'How stupid', she said, when I drew her attention to it. 'You see, I'm getting quite unused to wearing clothes like these since I joined the Movement.'

I find it interesting to recall this incident for that night Madame must have been making one of her last appearances in fashionable society. By the following year, 1909, she had turned her back forever on the gay life she had once led in art circles in Paris and in London and Dublin society.

A few years after that first meeting Madame moved away from County Dublin, and went to live in Surrey House, on Leinster Road, in Rathmines, and from 1911 on I became one of what was called 'the Surrey House clique', that is the circle of Madame's friends who were always in her company.

Although *Bean na h-Éireann* was meant to be a magazine for women, it was so well written and so outspoken on national and social questions, that it was soon circulating through Ireland, and even in the United States, and had as many or more men readers as it had women. Its editor was Miss Helena Moloney, the Abbey actress who later fought with the Citizen Army in 1916, and its staff included Madame Markievicz, Madame Gonne MacBride, Bulmer Hobson, Dr Patrick MacCartan, Sean MacGarry, Miss Madeleine ffrench-Mullen and myself.

Although we could pay neither staff nor contributors on *Bean na h-Éireann*, we had an impressive number of celebrities writing for us. Here are the names of some of these people who contributed regularly to our paper: James Stephens, George Russell, Arthur Griffith, Padraic Colum, Padraic O Conaire, Terence MacSwiney, Joseph Plunkett, Sir Roger Casement, Maeve Cavanagh, Seumus O'Sullivan, Count Markievicz, Susan Mitchell, Maud Gonne and Katherine Tynan.

We carried on a sort of bloodless guerrilla war against the British Empire. It filled our lives with excitement, gaity and good comradeship. At one stage a literary contribution to *Bean na h-Éireann* led to a serious crisis on the paper.

We were running a serial story by Katherine Tynan called 'The Priest's Gallows'. It was a romantic tale of '98, with the usual stock characters: there was the young hero, an insurgent chief; there was a lovely rebel maid with whom he was in love; there was a gallant (but misguided) English officer, also in love with the girl. We had never seen the whole story as Katherine Tynan was sending us a chapter at a time. When the story neared its end a chapter arrived describing a battle between the insurgents and the redcoats, in which the hero was fatally wounded. Confident that he would be rescued in a subsequent chapter, recover from his wounds in another, and be happily married to the heroine in the last, we let the story run on for several months more. When the last instalment arrived we found to our horror that the insurgent was dead and buried and that the gallant English officer led the blushing rebel maid to the altar. This was a bomb-shell dropped on *Bean na h-Éireann*. We spent hours arguing over a way out of the difficulty, and at last decided that the only thing to do was to re-write the last chapter, rescuing the insurgent, carrying him away to a mountain fastness, and healing him of his wounds. By this piece of surgery we had him ready to appear, pale, but still undaunted, in time to claim his bride from the arms of the English officer...

Much of the literary material in *Bean na h-Éireann* is unsigned. There are pen-names covering identies I cannot remember, but I can recall the following:

'Armid' or 'Macha' was Madame Markievicz; 'Emer', 'E' or 'A Worker' was Helena Moloney, who also wrote the editorial notes; 'B' was Bulmer Hobson; 'Maidbh' was Maud Gonne; 'M. O'Callaghan' or 'Dectora' was Madeleine ffrench-Mullen; 'Seumus Cassidy' was Count Markievicz; 'John Brennan' or 'Sorcha Ní Hanlon' was myself. The permanent features in the paper were 'An Grianan', the children's column, edited by Madeleine ffrench-Mullen; 'Labour Notes', written by Helena Moloney; 'The Woman with the Garden', written by Madame Markievicz...

It was some time after I had begun working on *Bean na h-Éireann* that I met Madame Gonne MacBride, for though she was President of Inghinidhe na h-Éireann and was on the committee from the beginning, she was away in France when we started. I won't attempt to describe her beauty to you, except to say that I had never then and have never since seen anything to compare with it. She was like a goddess, a creature from another planet, and when she spoke you thought she must speak in oracles. But one night there she was – sitting across the committee table quite close to me, and talking in the most practical manner about a plan which she had very much at heart. This was to provide a hot midday meal for the poor children in the Dublin schools.

No one today would believe the opposition the Inghinidhe had to overcome before the scheme was adopted. The Dublin Corporation, knowing that many of the children were on the borderline of starvation, had agreed to strike a rate for the purpose, only to be told by their legal adviser that they could not do so without having legislation passed in the British Parliament. But that night Madame MacBride was very happy. She had been asked by Canon Kavanagh, of St Audoen's, to start the work in the schools of his parish. The Women's Franchise League agreed to help the Inghinidhe in serving the meals, and we were soon busy in this school.

I needn't tell you that the prospect of getting a big plate of hot Irish stew was a great attraction at that school, so much so that the poor parents in the neighbourhood began to transfer their children to St Audoen's, and we were asked to extend the school feeding to John's Lane.

Would you like to know the names of the voluntary waitresses who served those meals to the children? I give you these from memory: Madame Gonne MacBride, Miss Helena Moloney, Madame Markievicz, Mrs Con Curran (then Miss Helen Laird), Miss Madeleine ffrench-Mullen, my sister Muriel (aferwards Mrs Thomas MacDonagh), my sister Grace (afterwards Mrs Joseph Plunkett), and myself.

Those were happy and exciting years for me. I felt like someone who had been living in banishment and had at last returned to live among my own people.

Sydney Gifford Czira: *The Years Flew By*, pp. 48-53

SELECTIONS FROM *BEAN NA h-Éireann*
On Franchise

Much that has been said and written on the subject of women's franchise and the national question, seem to have brought to light many people who do not blush to advise you to sacrifice principle to expediency as soon as the temptation occurs.

We hold in the first place that principle cannot be too high, and that uncompromising people, who are prepared to stick to their principles, cannot do either Sinn Féin or any other movement any harm.

Surely compromise never gives the impression of strength in a movement, and, therefore, when a Sinn Féiner starts an agitation to try and force the Parliamentary Party to do their best to pass a bill for them they at once weaken the Sinn Féin position by tacitly admitting, that once it comes to a vital issue, it is the Parliamentary Party that can give them their end not Sinn Féin.

If we are convinced that Sinn Féin is the one party that can free our Nation, if we believe all that Sinn Féiners have said and written for years, that agitation and organisation in this country is the only way to force England to restore us our National freedom, surely it seems going against all common sense, to suddenly turn to the Parliamentary Party, which has so often been dubbed 'The tail of the English Liberals' – consequently wagged by them – to turn to the Party as the people who can get us what we want.

Now we do not 'refuse to join the Woman's Franchise Movement' in the emphatic way that Maire nic Shuibne suggests, but we decline to join with Parliamentarians and Unionists in trying to force a bill through Westminister. We prefer to try and organise a woman's movement on Sinn Féin lines or on lines broader still. Freedom for our nation and the complete removal of all disabilities to our sex will be our battle cry.

April 1909

A reply to a paper read to Sinn Féin by a member of the Irishwomen's Franchise League represented the attitudes of the majority of Inghinidhe members.

The women of Irish Ireland have the franchise, and it would only be humiliating themselves and their country to appeal or even demand the endorsement of a hostile Parliament. They stand on equal footing with the men in the Gaelic League, in Sinn Féin, and the Industrial Movement. They are represented on the executives of all these, and under the present circumstances we should be content to regard these as representing Irish Government. The fact that they have not received the imprimatur of a hostile Government will worry no Nationalist woman. These movements leave plenty of room for the activities of Irish women, and if Sinn Féiners desire to forward their propaganda, they can elect women to any position they wish in spite of the British Government.'

Mary McLarren, April 1909

Physical Force

Physical force is here. Ireland is ruled by it, held by the throat, strangled and dáily sinking out of existence under its rough and relentless hands. Physical force is here and it is because we have ignored it, and neglected to use that power that God has given us for the upholding of our Nation, that we are in so poor a plight today.

Then let Irishmen recognise their duty and set themselves at last to the heavy task that is before them....A 'Moral Force' movement, ie a movement that stops short of shedding blood, and therefore forbids you to make the last sacrifice – that of your life – cannot be taken very seriously, and must end in contempt and ridicule.

September 1909

Dublin Gas

We would like to draw attention to the extraordinary attitude of the Dublin Gas Company towards women. They seem to drag the question of sex even into gas meters. One of our staff who wished to have gas laid on in premises taken by her gave the name of a lady friend as guarantee, when, to her astonishment, she was told that a lady would not be accepted as surety. Naturally we think the word of a woman quite as good as the word of a man, and we are glad to say that our colleague promptly decided to have electricity in the premises, with the result that an up-to-date Municipal enterprise is supported instead of a private company who holds early Victorian views about women.

October 1909

Editorial

We want our voice heard in Ireland. Alas it does not arrest the attention of the ordinary Anglicised citizen of this country, still less we fear does it appeal to the average woman. But time will change that, and the time will come when every woman in Ireland will believe as *Bean na h-Éireann* does that National and Separate Independence is our heritage and is to be won, and won only, by the courage of our hearts and the strength of our aims. We give our hand in comradeship to every worker for Irish freedom, or what they conceive to be freedom, whether it is sex emancipation, repeal of the Union, Home Rule, or even what is now called Home Rule. We are with them as long as Ireland and her welfare are first in their thoughts.

In our two years of existence as a journal we know we have done something towards keeping that hope alive in others. Indirectly we have benefitted our own sex, inasmuch as that the expression of militant nationalism by women must do much to command the respect of men and compel them to readjust their views on women as a possible force in the fight against foreign domination.

June 1910

WOMEN, IDEALS AND THE NATION
This lecture was delivered by Countess Markievicz to the Students National Literary Society, Dublin. It was published as a pamphlet by Inghinidhe na h-Éireann in 1909 and reissued by Cumann na mBan in 1918. In part an argument against nationalists taking up the suffrage cause, it is also uncompromising in its hope that armed rebellion will soon become a reality.

I take it as a great compliment that so many of you, the rising young women of Ireland, who are distinguishing yourselves every day and coming more and more to the front, should give me this opportunity. We older people look to you with great hopes and a great confidence that in your gradual emancipation you are bringing fresh ideas, fresh energies and above all a great genius for sacrifice into the life of the nation.

Now, I am not going to discuss the subtle psychological question of why it was that so few women in Ireland have been prominent in the national struggle, or try to discover how they lost in the dark ages of persecution the magnificent legacy of Maeve, Fheas, Macha and their other great fighting ancestors. True, several women distinguished themselves on the battle fields of '98, and we have the women of the *Nation* newspaper, of the Ladies' Land League, also in our own day the few women who have worked their hardest in the Sinn Féin movement and in the Gaelic League and we have the women who won a battle for Ireland, by preventing a wobbly Corporation from presenting King Edward of England with a loyal address. But for the most part our women, though sincere, steadfast Nationalists at heart, have been content to remain quietly at home, and leave all the fighting and the striving to the men.

Lately things seem to be changing ... so now again a strong tide of liberty seems to be coming towards us, swelling and growing and carrying before it all the outposts that hold women enslaved and bearing them triumphantly into the life of the nation to which they belong.

We are in a very difficult position here, as so many Unionist women would fain have us work together with them for the emancipation of their sex and votes – obviously to send a member to Westminster. But I would ask every nationalist woman to pause before she joined a Suffrage Society or Franchise League that did not include in their programme the Freedom of their Nation. A Free Ireland with No Sex Disabilities in her Constitution should be the motto of all Nationalist Women. And a grand motto it is.

Women, from having till very recently stood so far removed from all politics, should be able to formulate a much clearer and more incisive view of the political situation than men. For a man from the time he is a mere lad is more or less in touch with politics, and has usually the label of some party attached to him, long before he properly understands what it really means ...

Now, here is a chance for our women. Let them remind their men, that their first duty is to examine any legislation proposed not from a party point of view, not from the point of view of a sex, a trade or a class, but simply and only from the standpoint of their nation. Let them learn to be statesmen and not merely politicans. Let them consider how their action with regard to it may help or hinder their national struggle for independence and nothing else, and then let them act accordingly. Fix your mind on the ideal of Ireland free, with her women enjoying the full rights of citizenship in their own nation, and no one will be able to side-track you, and so make use of you to use up the energies of the nation in obtaining all sorts of concessions – concessions too, that for the most part were coming in the natural course of evolution, and were perhaps just hastened a few years by the fierce agitations to obtain them.

If the women of Ireland would organize the movement for buying Irish goods more, they might do a great deal to help their country. If they would make it the fashion to dress in Irish clothes, feed on Irish food – in fact, in this as in everything, *live really Irish lives*, they would be doing something great, and don't let our clever Irish colleens rest content with doing this individually, but let them go out and speak publicly about it, form leagues, of which 'No English goods' is the war-cry ...

I daresay you will think this all very obvious and very dull, but Patriotism and Nationalism and all great things are made up of much that is obvious and dull, and much that in the beginning is small, but that will be found to lead out into fields that are broader and full of interest. You will go out into the world and get elected onto as many public bodies as possible, and by degrees through your exertions no public institution – whether hospital, workhouse, asylum or any other, and no private house – but will be supporting the industries of your country...

To sum up in a few words what I want the Young Ireland women to remember from me. Regard yourselves as Irish, believe in yourselves as Irish, as units of a nation distinct from England, your Conqueror, and as determined to maintain your distinctiveness and gain your deliverance. Arm yourselves with weapons to fight your nation's cause. Arm your souls with noble and free ideas. Arm your minds with the histories and memories of your country and her martyrs, her language and a knowledge of her arts, and her industries. And if in your day the call should come for your body to arm, do not shirk that either.

May this aspiration towards life and freedom among the women of Ireland bring forth a Joan of Arc to free our nation!

Constance de Markieivcz: *Women, Ideals and the Nation*, 1909

NATIONALISM AND FEMINISM:
A FEMINIST CRITIQUE
Amongst the feminists who refused to join Inghinidhe na h-Éireann was Hanna Sheehy-Skeffington. In 1908 she co-founded the militant suffrage group, the Irish Women's Franchise League. Her analysis of the subordinate role occupied by women within the national movement provided the spark for much debate between the opposing views.

We all, Unionists and Nationalists, live overmuch on our past in Ireland. Our great past condones our empty present, and seems to deprecate, instead of stimulating endeavours. Living thus in our past, one is apt to overdraw one's bank account. This tendency is nowhere more aptly illustrated than with regard to the position of Irishwomen in the Ireland of to-day. Nowhere in the pitiful tangle of present-day life does the actual more sadly belie the far-off past. It is barren comfort for us Irishwomen to know that in ancient Ireland women occupied a prouder, freer position than they now hold even in the most advanced modern states, that all professions, including that of arms, were freely open to their ambitions ... that their counsel was sought in all affairs of state ... Our ancestresses were the state-recognized arbiters in matters under dispute between rival factions, forming a final court of appeal, a permanent Hague Tribunal.

'Where is it now, the glory and the dream?' Does the vision of the past mitigate the abject present? Is the degradation of the average

Irishwoman the less real, her education sacrificed to give her brothers ample opportunities of having a good time loitering through their examinations in the capital, her marriage a matter of sordid bargaining, broken maybe because an over-insistent prospective father-in-law demands a cow or a pig too much, her 'fortune' ... handed over blindly to her husband to dispose of it as he may think fit ...

I have chosen but a few salient examples to illustrate the disabilities Irishwomen suffer today. The result of Anglicization? This is but partly true; much of the evil is, however, inherent in latter-day Irish life. Nor will the evil disappear, as we are assured, when Ireland comes to her own again, whenever that may be. For until the women of Ireland are free, the men will not achieve emancipation. It is for Irishwomen therefore to work out their own 'Sinn Féin' on their own lines, for with the broader, non-party aspect of Sinn Féin – namely the reformation from within outwards, all Nationalists have always been in agreement.

The Irishwoman has far to go before achieving her destiny. At present she counts for less in her own land than does the Englishwoman in hers (time and again the Englishwoman has forced her point of view on reluctant legislators, and we may expect her one of these days to wrest the vote similarly from her countrymen). First, as the Englishwoman counts less to the nation than the Frenchwoman, and as the Frenchwoman is a harem-slave compared with her American sister, so in the scale of civilization the Irishwoman comes somewhere between the Oriental woman and her more advanced Western sisters.

Many vested interests (notably that of the publican) are openly opposed to any broadening of woman's horizon in Ireland. Public opinion, educational fallacies, convention militates against her assuming her rightful place in public life. In the Gaelic movement, in the Industrial revival and in the Sinn Féin organisation she has undoubtedly made her power felt. So much the better for the movement. The reason, however, is obvious; it is not due, as many would have us believe, to a reversion to the older Irish (for the individual in all these movements is as narrow as his presumably less enlightened brother), but rather because of the nature of the work involved. The Gaelic League must make its final appeal to the young, unless those to whom the very beginning are entrusted to take up Irish it will surely perish. So too with the Industrial revival – it is the woman who looks after the domestic budget, her voice can make or mar Irish Industrialism. Therefore, it is primarily in her capacity as mother and housekeeper, not as individual citizen, that these movements have of necessity recognised her importance. After all, as a wag has put it, 'woman is matchless as wife and mother'. No male has ever denied her these onerous privileges, and for that very reason the average male would see her confined to these purely incidental avocations. That is why, doubtless, many worthy Gaelic Leaguers get restive at the thought of women having places on the Executive Body, that is why, too, in spite of theoretical equality, some Sinn Féiners have not yet rounded Cape Turk where women are concerned. One of the leaders afforded an interesting object lesson to his women colleagues in the movement by founding university scholarships from which girls were expressly excluded. Irishwomen may be excused, therefore, if they distrust all parties in Ireland, for what I have said of the Sinn Féin organisation applies with far greater force to the Parliamentarian movement which, since the extinction of the Ladies' Land League in the eighties, has steadily ignored Irishwomen, hitherto indeed with impunity. It is for Irishwomen of every political party to adopt the principle of Sinn Féin in the true sense of the word and to refuse any longer to be the camp-followers and parasites of public life, dependent on caprice and expediency for recognition. It is for Irishwomen to set about working out their political salvation. Until the Parliamentarian and the Sinn Féin woman alike possess the vote, the keystone of citizenship, she will count but little with either party, for it is through the medium of the vote alone that either party can achieve any measure of success. This is a fact of which we Parliamentarians have long been aware to our cost, but which Sinn Féin women have yet to learn.

Hanna Sheehy-Skeffinton: *Bean na h-Éireann*, November 1909

CHAPTER 3

The Formation of
Cumann na mBan

'TO THE YOUNG WOMEN OF IRELAND'
The following article, published in a journal associated with the physical force tradition of nationalism, was one of the first to urge women to come forward to support the cause. It was written just as the Irish Volunteers were being formed.

Thousands upon thousands of you, young Irishwomen, do not realise that there is on foot in your country a great and lofty enterprise which needs your help. You grow up and let your youth pass without ever recognising that it is your duty to give it to her. There are few of you who do not learn, as part of your education, some fragment of your country's history and there are few of you, outside the definitely anti-national classes, who do not give at least a tacit adhesion to the Irish side in the struggle which has been going on for more than seven centuries to decide whether the Irish or the English shall rule in Ireland.

But this tacit adhesion is of very little use to the cause of national freedom as long as you do not take part in the fight yourselves.

Some of you may have read an article in the October number of *Irish Freedom*, calling on the young men of Ireland to prepare themselves for the call to fight for their nation's liberty, which may some day come suddenly to them.

If you did read it, you probably felt that it had nothing to do with you, that you, being women, could never be expected to bear arms for any cause, and that therefore you were a negligible quantity in the affairs of the nation.

It is assumed by a great many people, as a matter of course, that women cannot fight, but the merest glance backwards at history shows that there is not a country in the world, Ireland included, where women have not fought, and fought well, at one time or another. There were Boer women on the battlefields of South Africa twelve years ago, and please God, when the day comes for which 'Northman' in his article bàde the young men of Ireland prepare themselves, there will be women as well as men, ready to answer the

call. But whether you can fight or not, you are to the full as important
to Ireland and as much bound to her service, as your brothers and husbands are. The ways in which you can help are numerous, and the
ways in which you can, consciously and unconsciously, hinder her
progress towards freedom are also many. You can serve her by taking
part in the work of reviving the Irish language, or by consistently supporting native industries and manufactures, or by helping to organise
camogie clubs and girls' branches of Na Fianna Eireann, or by taking
part in the anti-enlistment campaign, or, so far as you have time and
power, in all three ways together. But if you want to be of use to
Ireland, you must not shy at the word 'politics'. You must be prepared to come forward as militant Nationalists (not 'constitutional'
Home Rulers) and to follow your principles openly, as men are
expected to do, even if they should lead you, through unpopularity
and the scorn of fashionable people, to the prison gate.

Ask yourselves the following questions, all of which but the last
were suggested by a branch of the Irish Industrial Development
Association, as an Irishwomen's Examination of Conscience:

Am I proud of my country and my people?
Do I know my country's history?
Do I help her industries?
Do I encourage Irish music, songs and dances?
Do I ridicule the use of the Irish language, the tongue which my
forefathers sang and spoke and did all their business in?
Do I ape the accent and style of the foreigner, while despising my
own national manners and customs?
Do I help any Institution or Association which has for its object
the improvement of Ireland?
Do I in any way which I could avoid, acquiesce in the British
occupation of Ireland?

The last question perhaps needs some explanation. To hold friendly
intercourse with soldiers or policemen, to sign addresses to British
royalty or to its representatives in Dublin, to take part in any fete or
gathering where the Union Jack is displayed or where any official of
the British Government is honoured in his (or her) official capacity, –
that is to acquiesce in the British occupation of Ireland, the forceful
domination of England over our country.

A girl whose living depends on the favour of unpatriotic employ-
ers cannot be expected to take part openly in patriotic work, but if she
can give satisfactory answers to the first seven of the above questions,
none of which seven border on politics, she is doing as much of her
duty to Ireland as her position will allow.

There is nothing unwomanly in active patriotism. Nobody calls Jeanne d'Arc unwomanly, nor Anne Devlin, nor, to come to our own times, Madame Maud Gonne nor the members of the Ladies' Land League; and whatever conservative-minded people may say to you now about the unseemliness of women actively and openly working for their country's cause: yet in the days when Ireland is free, no one will have anything but admiration for the women who contributed in however great or small a degree to the attainment of her freedom.

Southwoman: *Irish Freedom*, November 1913

WOMEN'S WORK IN THE VOLUNTEER MOVEMENT

The time-lag between the formation of the Irish Volunteers and the formation of its female counterpart, Cumann na mBan (Irishwomen's Council) was due to disagreement on whether the women would be part of the Volunteers, or whether they would be content to perform tasks like fund-raising when requested by the men. The article by Caitlin de Brun, published by the journal of the Volunteer movement, envisaged women's role to be totally subordinate to the needs of the Volunteers.

Are the women of Ireland as ready and willing to do their duty to their country as their Volunteer brothers? Will they do their part as nobly as the ladies of 1782, who made and ornamented flags and colours, embroidered uniforms with their own hands, contributed their trinkets and jewels to purchase ornaments and infused their own enthusiasm into the hearts of all ...

We can form ambulance corps, learn first aid, make all the flags to be carried by the Volunteers, do all the embroidery that may be required, such as badges on the uniforms, etc. Classes for women in first aid should be organised at once in every town where a corps of Volunteers has been formed. Trained nurses will be found almost everywhere whose services could be acquired to give lessons. Apart from the services we can render to the Volunteers, first aid should form part of every girl's training. Almost every town has its technical classes and girls have good opportunities of learning designing, drawing, etc. They will have a chance of putting their knowledge to practical use now in the making of flags for the Volunteers. To a patriotic Irishwoman could there be any work of more intense delight than that?

Caitlin de Brun: *Irish Volunteer*, 4 April 1914

INAUGURAL ADDRESS

The inaugural meeting of Cumann na mBan was presided over by Agnes O'Farrelly, whose depiction of the role to be played by women in the movement was couched in terms of an extension of their domestic responsibilities.

We have called this meeting of Irishwomen to meet the present national crisis, and to take measures for the liberty of the nation. We have here women of various opinions in national life, but they are ready, we believe, to merge their divergent views in face of the common danger.

There are many women present, to my knowledge, whom only the greatness and the imminence of the fiercest of the many struggles for independence waged in this island could have drawn from the shelter of their homes into the glare and possible turmoil attendant on a public utterance of the faith that is in them.

We may be told that it is not the business of women to interfere. Is anyone so stupid as not to see that the liberty or the enslavement of the nation affects every home and every individual, man and woman and child in the country?

Are the women to stand idly by whilst the dearest and most sacred things in life are at stake? Is the independence of the men of Ireland of no consequence to those who share their hearths and homes? If it is not our business then, in the name of Heaven, whose business is it?

Is not the liberty of the children of Ireland, the life-blood of the nation, at stake? Is not our own liberty – the liberty of the women of Ireland – wrapped up with the common liberty of the nation? Is not the interest of the men of this country our interest? With them we stand or fall. Is it our part, in the life of today, to remain with our heads thrust in the sand while the two great parties in the Imperial Parliament at Westminster keep alternately making moves in the game of British politics – a game in which Ireland is only a pawn – each move more dangerous than the other to our future peace and happiness?

Ireland, it seems to them, is caught in a cleft stick and dare not move. Recent events following rapidly on each other show us clearly that the time has come for Irishwomen to back up by every legitimate means the efforts of their countrymen. We have been watching anxiously for some time what for want of a better name I may call the cinematograph show in operation at present in the British House of Commons, and we are getting weary from the strain. The bewildering swiftness and completeness of the changes that take place in the political situation day by day makes one open the morning papers now with bated breath and in the full confidence that a beneficent

Parliament has provided a new thrill for the jaded public. The Grand National is not comparable now with Westminster if you want to bet on a chance. Yesterday it was Exclusion for Ulster, today it is an all-round Federal System. Tomorrow it will be a proposal to start migration from Munster to Ulster as a means of levelling things up. What next? Where do we come in?

We women are not in the thick of the fight, so we are untrammelled by the niceties of the situation.

We have, therefore, come here today to declare for the integrity of the nation, and for its inalienable right to self-government. We have come here to pledge ourselves to advance in every way in our power the liberty of Ireland. We offer our homage to the integrity and patriotism of the men who have given up the best years of their life to the fight initiated by Moore and Butt and Parnell; we offer our homage to the men who on Irish soil are forming the nucleus of a great Volunteer force for purposes of national defence and to back up and add the crowning triumph to the work of our representatives. We do not want a divided Ireland. We know the endless misery and recriminations that will be our legacy to generations yet unborn if we agree to the division of the country. Neither do we want an arrangement that will leave us unsettled for years, and that at the very time when stability is an absolute essential to laying the foundations of successful government. But, above all, we do not want Sir Edward Grey's suggested Federal system – a system which aims the cruellest and most wanton blow of all at the idea of unity and nationhood. The division to be created under the suggested exclusion by vote carries with it the possibility of final unity. The division created by a Federal Parliament in Dublin and another in Belfast is planned to be perpetual. That is the situation as it seems to me at the present moment. What can we women do to help, or must we allow our liberties and our future to be bartered to the Imperial interests of the moment? Our Provisional Committee in framing the rules of the Cumann na mBan or Irishwomen's Council, have outlined a scheme of work the details of which can be elaborated by the various branches of the organisation which, we have no doubt, will be at once formed throughout the country. Indeed in many centres the women are clamouring to be allowed to take a share in the long-drawn out struggle for liberty and nationhood. The hearts of the women are in the work. They only want to be organised. Wherever the men of Ireland are fighting for liberty they will not hesitate to help them. From the very nature of things the role of the women will be different from that of the men, and rightly so. It is not ours to undertake physically and directly the defence of the nation except in a last extremity and in the direct stress of war; yet, if such call were to come, I have no hesitation in saying that the spirit which animated the women of Limerick when they took the place of the men in the undefended breach is as much alive in Ireland to-day as it was two hundred years ago. Our first duty is to give our allegiance and support to the men who are fighting the cause of Ireland, whether in the British House of Commons or at home here in Ireland organizing National Volunteer corps. They are both fighting the national battle, and one is the complement of the other. Mr Churchill the other day declared that 200,000 men could be raised by National Ireland. He is right and it will be our privilege to help show him how true his estimate is. We women are not politicans, but we know what we want, and we are ready to work for it through thick and thin. Federation indeed! I was down in Ulster lately, in fact, I am in close and constant touch with Ulster and the feeling of Nationalists, moderate, sensible men and women, such as parish priests and councillors and mothers of families, is dead against any division of the country which might become permanent; and such an end, they say, to all their hopes and struggles is unthinkable. The exigencies, the fears and the turmoil of the present moment has brought here today women who until now were only known as home-makers. They are here because they fear for the liberty of the home, and because they realise that the blow aimed at the freedom of the men of Ireland strikes the women and children as well; our cause is a common cause, our interests are inextricably found together. In a moment of stress like the present that fact stands clear and unquestionable before us, and we realise the sacredness of the duty that impels us forward to the help of our common country. We have considered ways and means to that end, and our Provisional Committee have come to the conclusion that our first and immediate duty is to help toward the National Volunteer movement in our midst. We see plainly that an untrained and unarmed people are but a weak and defenceless mob, and it is due to our national self-respect to organise and equip these Volunteer companies which have arisen almost spontaneously as the outward and visible expression of a long dormant idea. Then if there were no Ulster question, there is a crying need for the Volunteers. Whatever laws we may be allowed to make will be but the make-believe of children whose elders allow them to play for the moment at independence. We pledge ourselves here today to give this cause our support morally, financially, and in every way we can. Let this be distinctly understood. We shall do ourselves the honour of helping to arm and equip our National Volunteers. Each rifle we put in their hands will represent to us a bolt fastened behind the door of some Irish home to keep out the hostile stranger. Each cartridge will be a watchdog to fight for the sanctity of the hearth. We shall start first-aid classes, and later on, if necessary, ambulance corps. Our constitution which will be formally placed before you embodies that idea and makes clear that the interests and the liberty of the nation we love and reverence will come first with us in this organisation. In so far as politics are the history of the moment, and our actions must be guided by events arising out of them we are political; otherwise we shall take no part in sectional politics, nor shall we take up the time of what is meant to be a purely practical organisation in discussing them. The surest way to prevent future discussion which might cause disunion among a body of women, all working in their various ways for the one great end of nationhood, is, it seems to me, to be perfectly frank at the outset as to the immediate circumstances which called us into existence. Four months ago we came together twice to discuss the formation of a Society and it did not seem to us then opportune. We feared to hamper whilst we were anxious to help. Events have occured since which convince us that the necessity for action on our part is urgent and a duty we owe ourselves and our country. We are going on, God helping us, without fear, knowing our cause to be right. Needless to add, we shall welcome as members and sisters in work every Irishwoman who puts Ireland first and who believes it is worthy striving for the liberty and rights of our historic nation.

Agnes O'Farrelly: *The Irish Volunteer*, 18 April 1914

SUFFRAGISTS AND NATIONALISTS
Members of the Irish Women's Franchise League also attended the first meeting of Cumann na mBan. A bitterly sarcastic account of their intervention at the meeting was published by the newspaper of the Irish suffrage movement.

Three days later the 'Irishwomen's Council' assembled in the Mansion House to inaugurate a scheme by which rifles would be procured for the men for some undefined and undefinable end. The meeting opened with the skirl of Irish pipes on a war-like note. The generosity, the devotion and enthusiasm of Irishwomen were lauded; reference was made to the women of Limerick; we were reminded that 'our ancient Irish liberties' (whatever they are) were in peril, and that delicately-nurtured women whom wild horses (or wild geese?) could not drag from the sacred shelter of home and babies were flocking to the standard of Miss O'Farrelly, clamouring to hold collecting-boxes in the defence of home and motherland. The British Empire was spoken of in the scathing terms that only Fenians use, and the platform (boasting Government officials and female relatives of Liberal Ministers) beamed approval as if to England's National

Anthem. Nothing disturbed the even tenor of the subscription list.

Suddenly a 'Volunteer' speaker began to ask questions – awkward ones. Was the Irishwomen's Council to have a place in the Executive? What were the liberties that Irishwomen possessed? What did Irishwomen think of the Cat and Mouse Act and the Government that foisted this alien measure on their countrywomen?

Uproar ensued as Mrs Sheehy-Skeffington put these points; the men for whom rifles were to be procured at the sacrifice of 'fur coats' howled to have the insolent one put out; the chair explained that the liberties of Irishwomen did not form part of the constitution of the new society, and were entirely 'out of order'; that the only question of interest at present was buying rifles for men, and that nothing else was of the slightest importance to the truly womanly – and the 'unwomanly' in the audience smiled to themselves and thought deep thoughts on the nature of men who cannot buy a rifle unless a woman collects the money – women, the ministering angel of the ambulance-class, who provides the pyjamas and the lint, but who sinks below the human the moment she asks for a vote!

Irish Citizen, 9 May 1914

Heated exchanges concerning the relationship between Cumann na mBan and the Volunteer movement continued over several months in the pages of the Irish Citizen. *Rosamund Jacob, a Quaker from Waterford, urged for some moderation in the abuse being levelled by both sides.*

The writer of the leading article called 'The Slave Women Again' in last week's *Irish Citizen* attempts no answer to most of the points in Miss MacSwiney's article, but fastens on its one weak spot – the defence of Mr Redmond's anti-suffrage policy. I do not think this can be logically defended by any suffragist, for Mr Redmond has made it very plain that his attitude on the question is due at least as much to bitter and uncompromising enmity to the principle of sex equality as to the exigencies of his position. The *Irish Citizen* (very prudently, from its own point of view) ignores the rest of Miss MacSwiney's article, except her Anglo-German parallel, and its answer to that shows, in rather a painful way, the inability of the suffrage-first-at-any-price party to comprehend the meaning of patriotism.

It has been said, in justification of the *Irish Citizen*'s present policy, that there can be no free nation without free women. This is true in one sense. but the term 'a free nation' may be used in two different senses, either to express a nation of free citizens, or a nation free from foreign control; and a nation must be free in the latter sense before it can be free in the former. Political rights conferred on Irishwomen by a foreign government would be a miserable substitute for the same rights won, even three years later, from our own legislative assembly.

The *Irish Citizen* has two theories on this subject, to both of which it clings with dogged persistence. One is, that every nationalist is an obedient follower of Mr Redmond; and the other is, that so long as women have no votes, they have no duty to their country. The *Irish Citizen*'s idea of public duty is that we nationalists should abandon for an indefinite time, and even oppose, the cause of national liberty for the chance of getting the vote a few years earlier than we might otherwise get it. The woman who does this is a true suffragist, no doubt, but no one can call her a Nationalist.

I suppose no self-respecting woman will deny that the members of Cumann na mBan (unlike the *Irish Citizen* I prefer to use the Irish rather than the English form of its name) will be much to blame if they do not insist on their organi-sation being represented on the Volunteer executive, and that all possible pressure should be brought to bear on them to do so. But I do not think any Nationalist woman can be blamed for preferring the work of providing rifles for the Volunteers to being instructed, by Mrs Pethick-Lawrence or any other Englishwoman, as to the ideals of nationalism for which she should strive.

In a controversy like this, where neither side is really inimicable to the other, provocative terms of abuse like 'slave women' should be scrupulously avoided. The *Irish Citizen* has no more right to call Miss MacSwiney, and those who think with her, 'slave women', than Miss MacSwiney would have to call the Irish Citizen's party 'Irish traitors.'

I must apologise for the length of this letter, but before concluding it I want to say that the *Irish Citizen* sets a badly-needed example to most journals in being always ready to publish criticisms of its own policy.

Rosamund Jacob: *Irish Citizen*, 30 May 1914

THE ALLIES OF THE VOLUNTEERS
Membership of Cumann na mBan grew rapidly. By September, Mary Colum, who was one of its first organisers, felt confident enough to rebut the critics.

It is now on all sides acknowledged that Cumann na mBan – the Irishwomen's Council – is the most vigorous and enterprising of all the movements that have grown out of the idea of arming and drilling the nation. It started in a small way, and got but little newspaper advertisement – the founders of the movement deliberately avoided it – but now quite suddenly the realisation has forced itself on friends and foe of the Volunteer movement that this organisation of women is a force to be reckoned with, that it is growing with remarkable rapidity, for all the patriotic energies of the women of the country are rushing towards it.

The destiny of small nations always finally depends on their women. This is a truth that every leader of any movement in this country must take into account; it was fully realised by the great leader of the last victorious movement in Ireland – Michael Davitt – when he founded the Ladies' Land League as the last line of defence. It is a truth perfectly accepted by the young captains and secretaries of the Volunteers, who help us, of Cumann na mBan, to found our branches throughout the country. From the ranks of these young, daring and self-sacrificing men will come perhaps the great leader we are all looking for.

'If Ireland comes to anything among the nations of Europe,' said that most astute observer of national conditions, Dr Emil Reich, 'you may take it from me, though you may never read it in book or in newspaper, it will be through its women.' And so it was with a strong feeling that if the Volunteer movement was to be a great national one women must take their due place in it, that a few women gathered together in a small room to found the Cumann na mBan. At first a great many difficulties came in the way; when at last, after many meetings, the organisation was formed, it had no name but it had very definite aims. We stated the aims of our new-born political organisation thus:-

1. To advance the cause of Irish liberty
2. To organise Irishwomen in furtherance of this object
3. To assist in arming and equipping a body of Irish men for the defence of Ireland
4. To form a fund for these purposes, to be called the 'Defence of Ireland Fund'.

And so Cumann na mBan was launched. From the start it had in its body some of the gallant fighters of the Land League days – women who had worked hard in that great conquering movement and who saw in the new Volunteer force the salvation of Ireland. They were an inspiration to the younger women who brought their youth and strong faith and eagerness into the new fight. Soon branches began to be formed in the country, slowly at first, then more quickly until now at the moment of writing there are over half a hundred branches in

Ireland and several in England. Every day some body of women struggling by themselves in a country town to find an outlet for their patriotism and their desire to work for Ireland, realise that their place is in Cumann na mBan. And so steadily the movement grows and the spirit grows. Where the members of Cumann na mBan are the most numerous the spirit of the Volunteers is best. What are recognised as the best drilled and most efficient regiments in the country are backed by the strongest force of women.

From the start we of Cumann na mBan decided to do any national work that came within the scope of our aims. We would collect money or arms, we would learn ambulance work, learn how to make haversacks and bandoliers, we would study the question of food supplies, we would practice the use of the rifle, we would make speeches, we would do everything that came our way – nothing is too high or too low for us to attempt, for we are not the auxiliaries or the hand-maidens or the camp followers of the Volunteers – we are their allies. We are an independent body with our own executive and our own constitution. If some unhappy fate were now to destroy the Volunteers, Cumann na mBan is not only capable of still growing and flourishing, it is capable of bringing the whole Volunteer movement to life again. It has in its membership all forms of national opinion. It asks of no man or woman more than to acknowledge the ideas, subscribed to in these words by the Conservative and Unionist editor of the 'British Review': 'Ireland is not a Crown Colony, Ireland is a Nation.' We want the status and liberties of a nation, for the gaining and defending of which our Volunteers sprang into being. Irishmen have fought and fell in defence of every country in Europe. This time, we women of the new movement, ask the men to put all their thought and energies into gaining and defending the rights and liberties of their own country. Men or nations who are able to fight their own battles make such sought-for allies. Men who fight the battles of other people are either fools or mercenaries. We in Ireland have for too long been playing the fool and the mercenary, so that all our patriotic songs are beaten songs, the songs of a crushed people... In this year of grace 1914 let us 'wave a brand, and take our stand' within the four seas of our own country, to fight our own fight first, and this time we shall not be worsted in the game.

Mary Colum: *Irish Freedom*, September 1914

'BUY A REVOLVER'
The gulf between nationalist and feminist remained wide. Constance Markievicz, active in the Irish Citizen Army, made strong criticism of

the subordinate role of Cumann na mBan in a speech to the Irish Women's Franchise League in October 1915. It was a radical, idiosyncratic expression of liberated womanhood.

By a law passed at the Council of Drumleat, 590, the women of Ireland were exempted from military service. Over one hundred years later the law had to be renewed, as it had become inoperative! Ancient Ireland bred warrior women, and women played a heroic part in those days. Today we are in danger of being civilised by men out of existence. What distinguished Ireland chiefly of old was the number of fighting women who held their own against the world, who owed no allegiance to any men, who were the super-women – the Maeves, the Machas, the warrior-queens....

That spirit is now only alive in the suffragettes. Throughout later history, though Irishwomen have suffered and worked, they have as a rule taken no prominent part; there are no great leaders. Dervorgilla was a creature of sex simply. Granuaile, true, went back to the older type and was a fighting queen, but not much is known of her.

Countess Markievicz here touched on many of the women of '98, and pointed out how little is known of them. She went on to say that of all these we get glimpses from male chronicles, but their roles seem to have been passive. They followed and helped the men, they did not initiate enterprises of their own. The same is true even of brave Anne Devlin, true of weak Sarah Curran, who drifted to madness on Emmett's death, and married one of his bitter foes.

The Ladies' Land League, founded by Anna Parnell, promised better things. When the men leaders were all imprisoned it ran the movement and started to do the militant things that the men only threatened and talked of, but when the men came out, they proceeded to discard the women – as usual – and disbanded the Ladies' Land League. That was the last of women in nationalist movements, down to our time. Today the women attached to national movements are there chiefly to collect funds for the men to spend. These Ladies' Auxiliaries demoralise women, set them up in separate camps and deprive them of all initiative and independence. Women are left to rely on sex charm, or intrigue and backstairs influence.

Tommy Moore, the popular poet of his day and also many days later, has set Ireland a very low idea of woman to worship. To him, woman is merely sex and an excuse for a drink. Not a companion or a friend, but a beautiful houri holding dominion by her careful manipulation of her sex and her good looks... The better ideal for women who, whether they like it or not, are living in a work-a-day world, would be – If you want to walk round Ireland, or any other country, dress suitably in short skirts and strong boots, leave your jewels and gold wands in the bank, and buy a revolver. Don't trust to your 'feminine charm' and your capacity for getting on the soft side of men, but take up your responsibilities and be prepared to go your own way depending for safety on your own courage, your own truth and your own common sense, and not on the problematic chivalry of the men you may meet on the way. The two brilliant classes of women who follow this higher ideal are suffragettes and the Trades Union or Labour women. In them lies the hope of the future. But for them women are everywhere today in a position of inferiority. And the Churches, both Catholic and Protestant, are to blame for this, for both foster the tradition of segregation of the sexes.

A consciousness of their own dignity and worth should be encouraged in women. They should be urged to get away from wrong ideals and false standards of womanhood, to escape from their domestic ruts, their feminine pens. It would be well to aim at bringing out, as it were, the masculine side of women's souls, as well as the feminine side of men's souls. War is helping to do this by shaking women out of old grooves and forcing responsibilities on them. We have got to get rid of the last vestige of the Harem before woman is free as our dream of the future would have her.

Constance de Markievicz: *Irish Citizen*, 23 October 1915

CHAPTER 4

The Easter Rising

THE HOWTH GUN-RUNNING

Women contributed in many different ways to the preparations for the Easter Rising. One important task was smuggling weapons into Ireland. Mary Spring Rice made the suggestion of using yachts to bring the guns from Germany and she was one of the crew of the Asgard, *the yacht which had been a wedding present to Molly Childers from her parents. On 26 July 1914 the* Asgard, *sailed by Erskine Childers, his wife Molly, Mary Spring Rice, Gordon Shepherd and two Donegal fishing men, landed 900 guns and 29,000 rounds of ammunition at Howth Harbour. The following are extracts from the diary of Mary Spring Rice.*

Sunday 12th – As the tug came up Darrell Figgis called from her deck that Conor had taken 600 rifles and 20,000 rounds of ammunition. 'He's left you 900 and 29,000 rounds,' he shouted. We looked at each other. Could we ever take them? We had only counted on 750, and they looked enormous, each thickly done up in straw.

However, before we could say 'knife' we were all at work unloading. It was a perfect night, quite calm, the tug looked black and huge alongside us. Her deck was full of German sailors who jabbered away and looked curiously at us, as they passed down the big canvas bales to Pat and Duggan on our deck. I found myself in the saloon with Mr Gordon, Pat passing us down rifles through the skylight, and we packing them in, butts at the end and barrels in the centre, as fast as we could. They came in bales of ten, and we counted them as we stowed them – '8,9,10, steady a minute, Pat, till I stow this one.' Inside the cabin Erskine and Molly were doing the same thing. 40 went into the port bunk in the saloon, should we ever get them all in? 'We'll have to take the straw off and pack them singly if we're ever to take 900,' said Mr Gordon, so we shouted up to take the straw off. It was fearfully hot work; they were fairly heavy and thick with grease which made them horrible to handle. Gradually, however, the pile grew and presently the saloon was half full, level with the table; and we went up on deck to help strip straw off, as they could hardly hand them down fast enough. Then when we had undone a certain number –

49

below again to pack them in. So it went on through the night – still bale after bale of rifles were passed down from the tug, and every now and again we shouted to the German crew to know how many more were still to come, and the saloon got full, and the cabin and the passage, and then we began to put on another layer, and to pile them at the foot of the companion hatch. Meanwhile, the ammunition had been coming down in fearfully heavy boxes, which were stowed with infinite labour aft under the cockpit, a very difficult place to get at, at the foot of the companion, in the sail lockers, and a couple in the fo'castle. Erskine was very keen to take all the ammunition we possibly could, and certainly it seemed rather a sin to leave it to be put overboard by the tug, and aboard it all came somehow; several boxes were left on the deck till we could make room to stow them. Personally, I felt rather nervous as to the effect this tremendous extra weight would have on the yacht in bad weather, but Erskine's one thought was to take everything. As we toiled away I heard them saying we had drifted right down near the Ruytigen, the people there must have wondered what on earth we were doing, but there was no time to alter our position, only try to finish it before it got light, and a faint glimmer of dawn was beginning to show as we stowed away feverishly to get them in. Molly put pieces of chocolate literally into our mouths as we worked and that kept us going, till, about 2 a.m. the last box was heaved on to the deck and the last rifle shoved down the companion, and the captain of the tug came on board to have a drink and consult where he would tow us to.

SUNDAY 26TH – We had, of course, no news from the Provisional Committee for three weeks, and perhaps no Volunteers were coming down at all. We had to get in and out of Howth Harbour with the high tide so there wasn't much time for delays. As we got nearer I went down and cleared out the guns in our bunk, thinking as I laboured at them that if we had to put out again with them still on board what a dreary job it would be stowing them all back again. We were close by when I had finished and there was Howth pier plainly visible, and Molly gazing to see if any Volunteers could be seen. We all felt very doubtful about them for we couldn't think it was too rough for the motor boat to come out, and were afraid something had happened to make them give up the whole thing. However, as my red skirt was to be the signal, I stood well up on deck. It was no easy matter with a fresh breeze to lower the sails at just the right moment to run alongside the quay, when minutes might be so precious. Molly took the helm and Erskine and the men got the sails down, and joy, oh joy! there was a group of men on the pier-head to catch the rope. Duggan was a bit late throwing the warp and we shot on past the pier-head. But the men got hold of the rope and hauled her back alongside.

A quarter to one, up to time to the minute, and a long line of Volunteers were marching down the quay. There was Mr Gordon on the pier-head and, of course, the inevitable Figgis. Then things began to move. At first there was a fearful scramble among the men on shore for the rifles as they were handed up, then Erskine stopped the delivery until he got hold of someone in command and some sort of order was restored. Molly and I and Mr Gordon stood by the mizzen and looked at the scene; it still seemed like a dream, we had talked of this moment so often during the voyage.

> Mary Spring Rice: 'Diary of the *Asgard*, 1-26 July 1914', in (ed.) F X Martin: *The Howth Gun-Running*, pp. 79-80; 95.

'HAD I BEEN A BOY'

The Fianna, as the best trained section of the nationalist forces, were an important element in ensuring that the guns were landed and stored safely. For Nora and Ina, daughters of James Connolly, the deliberate manner in which they and Constance Markievicz were excluded from knowledge of the Howth guns was an unwelcome reminder that the sexes were not equal in everyone's eyes. They were amongst the few women in Constance Markievicz's youth organisation, Na Fianna Eireann.

In the summer of 1914 Nora and I were camping with the Countess Markievicz at her cottage on the Three Rock with a number of the boys of the Fianna. They all disappeared on Sunday morning, saying they had been invited out and no girls were welcome. We were to pass the day as best we could and they would be out in the evening to see us.

This was most unusual; even Madame had not been asked. We put in our time nicely with Madame, listening to her stories. In fact we were pleased to have her to ourselves for the day, as she was usually surrounded by young people making demands on her in one way or another.

When we heard that guns had been run in at Howth and us sitting pretty a few miles away, it nearly broke our hearts. How could we face up to Belfast and father and say we knew nothing and did less? It looked as if we were not to be trusted – we, who had been called upon at all times and under any circumstances, and had always turned to when wanted. Nora took me by the arm and led me away from the boys, telling me not to show my feelings so plainly. 'A good soldier takes disappointment and defeat with his chin up. Perhaps they wanted to leave somebody at the cottage in case they were all arrested.' This was poor comfort, but she did her best to heal the wound. 'Had I been a boy', I said, 'I should not have been overlooked.' 'Hush', Nora said, 'there is still tomorrow.'

The next day we were on the go from dawn till midnight, here, there and everywhere, delivering orders regarding the safety of the guns. When I heard I was to take small-arms to Belfast and was told of the consequence if we were stopped, it more than made up for the earlier disappointment.

The dear Countess said: 'You are the first women to run guns to the North. Show what you're made of. Deliver them safely is all I ask. I have every confidence in you.' She explained the plan: a Fianna member would drive up in his car. He would pretend to know nothing of what we were bringing and would deny anything we said. 'You must be prepared to take full responsibility', Madame told us, 'and if you're caught, you know nothing, heard nothing, but only got the chance of a lift home from your holidays with this stranger you met at a dance. Is that clear?' I told her it was and I assured her I would do my best.

How I counted the hours and miles! Motoring was new to me and this was my first long journey. We had not gone far when we encountered engine trouble, but the driver knew a good deal about his car and with some coaxing he got it going. Then there was some difficulty as to the right direction. We had to stop several times, as we found ourselves on the wrong road and had to turn back and retrace our path...

We arrived safely and it was dark and bringing the guns to our house was simple. Father was there to greet us and slap us on the back. 'Bravo, and well done. I could not have done better myself.' That was a good trait in father – he was never slow in giving us praise if we deserved it. I believe it goes a long way with the young to know they are appreciated by their elders.

In a couple of days we knew how to handle a gun. We had a large bedroom that took in the sitting room and the hall. One could lie full-length on the floor and have plenty of room to play in, even though the gun was long and clumsy. At Christmas we had a shooting competition, and we gave a turkey to the winner. It was won by Miss Roisin Walsh, late Dublin City Librarian, who made a present of it to our family, as she had no need to take one home to the country. It was a generous act on her part.

Ina Connolly-Heron: 'James Connolly – A Biography'. *Liberty*, August 1966

PREPARATIONS

The experience of Maire nic Shuibhlaigh was typical of many Cumann na mBan members in the weeks before the Rising. In a role similar to those women who supported the British war effort against Germany, their major task was to prepare medical kits.

I had begun a small branch of Cumann na mBan at Glasthule – about twenty members, whose homes were in the vicinity. There was little for us to do locally at the time, but we occupied the evenings with first aid lectures and occasional visits from Ard Craobh (central branch) visitors. Most of the time during the early months of 1916 was taken up with the endless preparation of medical kits for Volunteers which, with those made by other Cumann na mBan branches, were sent to areas throughout the country.

During Holy Week, 1916, I spent the days making up these kits at the Volunteer headquarters in Dawson Street. Most branches in the city had been notified of a coming route march to the country on Easter Sunday, and preparations for this were under way.

On Easter Sunday I visited some friends, the Ceannts, at their home in Dolphin's Barn. Both Mrs Ceannt and her sister, Lily O'Brennan, were active members of the central branch of Cumann na mBan. They had both spent the afternoon preparing first-aid kits and assembling equipment for the 4th Dublin Battalion of Volunteers of which Eamon Ceannt was commandant. Lily asked me what arrangements I had made for the proposed route march. 'None, as yet,' I told her, adding that the Glasthule Cumann na mBan had not, to my knowledge, been notified of its part in the arrangements and might not go at all. She said that next afternoon she was moving off with Eamonn's battalion and asked if I would like to go with her. I said yes. 'Be here at three o'clock tomorrow afternoon, and bring your bicycle,' she said.

We made no further reference to this arrangement. I never thought to ask where the battalion would meet, or where it would go afterwards. It was natural to assume that we would move off to the hills and spend the day there in manoeuvres. No one knew that the route march was really a covert manner of mobilising for an insurrection. On Monday morning this ignorance of the whereabouts of Ceannt was to leave me completely uncertain of what was taking place in the city, and to cut me off completely from his battalion, which subsequently took the South Dublin Union buildings at Mount Brown and held them with many skirmishes and bitter fighting until the announcement of surrender by Pearse.

Maire Nic Shiubhlaigh: *The Splendid Years*, pp. 161-2

A few women, mainly female relatives of the leaders, were given important tasks to perform in the few days before the Rising.

Early in April, Tom and Sean MacDermott asked me to select sixteen girls, members of Cumann na mBan, for despatch work, girls whose silence and discretion they could absolutely rely upon. With the help of Miss MacMahon I drew up a list and handed it to Tom, and I have the intense satisfaction that all were true to the trust placed in them.

On Palm Saturday night, 1916, the Central Branch of Cumann na mBan held a Ceilidhe (dance) in, I think, the Grocer's Hall, Parnell Square. Many criticised us for having it on such a night, but I had been asked by Sean MacDermott to hold it in order to cover a meeting with men from the provinces. Miss MacMahon and I got busy to carry out his request, and we were the only two in the branch who knew the object of the Ceilidhe. Sean came early, and asked me to stay with him until those he had to meet turned up, as he could leave me without apology. I asked if he would mind Miss MacMahon staying with us. He said, 'If you wish, I have no objection. She will of course understand when I leave you.' So we both formed a kind of bodyguard for him; many of his friends who would, I knew, have liked to speak to him passed into the hall, but with Miss MacMahon on one side of him and myself on the other they did not dare...

Con Colbert came into the shop to protest against a Ceilidhe being held in Lent. He was deeply religious, and did not think it right. I could not explain the reason for it to him, so I told him not to be so squeamish and to dance while he could, as he might be dancing at the end of a rope one of these days. I fear I shocked him, and I was sorry the minute the words were out of my mouth. I was sorry for being so flippant, but I was under a great strain at the time.

I had no intimate knowledge of the work of the other branches of Cumann na mBan in Dublin or throughout the country, but I did know, as a member of the Executive, that they all worked as hard as Central Branch, of which I was President.

On the Tuesday of Holy Week, 1916, Tom left the shop in Parnell Street to go to a meeting. I took his place there, and when he was not back by 11 pm I closed the shop and went home, hoping to find him there. He was not and after a while I began to worry. It was unusually late for him. Our house was at the end of the avenue, which was not well lighted, and I was always uneasy when he was late, fearing that some night the British might lay for him there and murder him...

On reaching home we settled to supper, and during it he told me the great news, that the Rising had been arranged for the following Sunday, that a Proclamation had been drawn up to which he was first signatory. I said 'That means you will be first President'. 'Yes,' he said, 'that is what it means.' Then he told me how the Proclamation was drawn up. Some time before, Pearse had been asked to draft it on lines intimated to him and submit it to the Military Council. He did, and some changes were made. When it was signed that night, it represented the views of all except one, who thought equal opportunities should not be given to women. Except to say that Tom was not that one, my lips are sealed.

On Holy Thursday, I was sent to Limerick with despatches. I took my three children with me to leave them with my mother, so that I could be free to take on the duty assigned to me in the Rising.

Helen Litton (ed.): *Revolutionary Women: Kathleen Clarke*, pp. 68-9, 71.

THE EASTER RISING
Given the confusion of orders and countermanding orders that characterised the start of the Rising, many women found that their branches of Cumann na mBan had been forgotten about. They had to find a way to the various outposts alone; crossing streets that had become dangerous and pleading with Volunteer officers to be allowed to join the garrison.

JACOB'S FACTORY
In Harcourt Street the door of the Sinn Féin office was open and five girls stood in the hallway. One, Sara Kealy of the Fairview Cumann na mBan, I knew by sight; another was named Kathleen Lane. There were two sisters named Pollard and a girl named Annie McQuade.

A man ran down the street. Passing the door, he called over his shoulder: 'The Citizen Army are taking the Green! The Volunteers are breaking into Jacob's factory!'

Sara, who did not look very old – about seventeen – said: 'I've been to Jacob's. I saw one of the Volunteers. I think Tom MacDonagh's there!'

The factory was about three minute's walk away. We set off down the road...

As we turned the corner opposite Jacob's, a huge crowd of poorly-dressed men and women, some of them shouting and screaming and waving fists, came into view. Later we learned that this was a mixed crowd of Jacob's factory employees and 'Separation Allowance' women – the wives of British soldiers fighting in France. They were quarrelling together on the footpaths. As we pushed on we saw the caps of Volunteers bobbing over the heads of the crowd, and caught the glint of steel. Then we were under the side of Jacob's.

An armed guard stood at the gate ignoring the shrieks of the crowd. We went up to him and told him who we were. 'I don't know what you should do,' he said. 'You'd better go over to that gate and get inside.'

Just inside a door, in a passageway which appeared to lead to the main bakery of the building, I met Tom MacDonagh in the full uniform, cloak cap and accoutrements of a Volunteer commandant. He was talking to Major MacBride who was still in civilian clothes, a navy-blue suit, grey hat, a malacca walking-cane on his arm.

MacDonagh said: 'My God ... It's Máire Walker! How did you get in?' . He put down his head, shaking it from side to side. A typical gesture. He seemed very much at ease.

After a while he said: 'We haven't made any provisions for girls here.'

I explained that we could cook for the garrison and look after casualties. He asked how many of us there were. I told him: 'Only six', and asked if I would go and see if any others had arrived in Sinn Féin. 'Yes', he said 'but hurry.'

There were no more girls at Harcourt Street. Most of the Cumann na mBan members had already moved off with their respective companies. I returned to Jacob's ...

Looking out towards the Peter Street side of the building, near the Adelaide Hospital, we were just in time to witness a striking incident. A group of Volunteers were letting the remainder of their comrades into the building. Down the street, swaying from side to side, came an open two-seater car. As it drew abreast of Jacob's a figure in Citizen Army uniform stood up in the front seat and waved its hat above its head. It was Madame Markievicz on her way to Stephen's Green.

'Go at it, boys!' she yelled. 'The Citizen Army are taking the Green! Dublin Castle is falling!'

On the first or second floor, reached from the bakery by a steel staircase, we found a perfectly-equipped but useless kitchen, formerly equipped by gas and electricity. Three Volunteers disconnected a couple of immense copper boilers and carried them down to the forge where we set them on the fire. They made excellent urns for boiling meat and vegetables and brewing tea. Despite constant foraging through the building this first day no food suitable for hungry men could be found. There were biscuits in plenty, 'plain and fancy' – mostly fancy – slabs of rich fruit-cake, some shortbread and a few tons of cream crackers. But there was nothing of which to make a hot drink. Eventually one of the girls found a gross or two of slab cooking chocolate. It was grated into the biggest boiler and stewed until it melted. The result was a dark-brown cocoa-like syrup, taken without sugar or milk. It looked horrible, but at least it was sustaining.

Though calls could be heard from the upstairs rooms, the sound of footsteps, an occasional clatter as a rifle fell, there was an eeriness about the place; a feeling of being cut off from the outside world.

As the evening drew to a close, a hush settled on the factory, broken only by the occasional crack of rifles overhead or in the distance. When darkness settled, a group of Volunteers entered the bakeroom with candles which they set about the room in empty biscuit boxes. The boxes faced inwards, away from the windows, forming a huge circle; intensifying the darkness beyond. There was a murmur of voices from the doorway, and men started to shuffle into the light. The whole garrison, with the exception of those on sentry-duty, gathered inside the circle and knelt. Someone started the Rosary ...

Looking back now to the Rising, trying to remember different incidents, it is not easy to recall all that went on around us in Jacob's. Quartered downstairs, we had long, busy periods, for our party was small, and there was much to be done ... Everyone had their own work to do and no one was certain of what went on elsewhere. For us downstairs the work would be broken by long periods of waiting, which were really the worst feature of our time in the building ... I spent most of the day downstairs, for MacDonagh had forbidden us the freedom, unescorted, of the upper parts of the building, where a figure passing a window at once became a target of British bullets. The only time we left the ground floor was to attend his headquarters for instructions. Later in the week he relaxed this order and I climbed to one of the roof-towers from where I saw the last of the burning GPO.

The pity was that it ended so soon. The news of the surrender, when it came, was heartbreaking.

Tom MacDonagh came in. He climbed onto a table and held up his hand. The noise died away at once.

He said, very sadly: 'We have to give in. Those of you who are in civilian clothes, go home. Those in uniform stay on. You cannot leave if you are in uniform.' He stepped down...

I gave the girls MacDonagh's order. They did not want to leave. I could understand their feelings. They were my own; I did not want to go, myself. I told them what MacDonagh had said. He was anxious to have all girls out of the building before he surrendered. He feared that we would be arrested. If this had been the only consideration, I would have ignored his plea, and stayed; but he thought that the sight of the girls being arrested might upset the men – he wanted everything to go as quietly as possible. On the other hand, Sara Kealy said that it might be useful for a few girls to stay behind. They could write letters for the men and take messages to relatives. I did not press the matter.

In the midst of much confusion, some women in Cumann na mBan uniform came in; amongst them Louise Gavan-Duffy and Min Ryan from the GPO. They were on their way home and asked me to go with them. MacDonagh came through the crowd and asked, 'Will you go now, please?'

'I don't know, Tom. All the girls insist on staying.'

MacBride was standing just inside one of the exits. 'It would be better for you to go,' he said. As we shook hands, he asked that a message be taken to some friends at Glasthule. 'Tell them, too, that we had a good week of it,' he added simply.

Outside, a British officer was standing near one of the gateways. He said, 'I'll see you over the roadway, ladies.'

We walked down the roadway and turned the corner into Camden Street. It was a route I had taken many times through the years. I cannot remember what we talked about – if we talked at all, for there did not seem very much to say. I felt confused and disappointed. All at once, I had begun to feel very tired.

Along Camden Street the shop windows were shuttered and dark. We passed few people on the footpath. Everything looked strange, even the street was different. It was as though I had never seen it before.

Despite what was going on inside, Jacob's looked very dark, very empty. Dublin seemed unnaturally still.

Máire Nic Shiubhlaigh: *The Splendid Years*, pp. 166-86

A VIEW FROM THE STREETS

Soon after we were married came the Rebellion. I remember that Easter Monday: the weather was great. You could have fried a rasher on the ground. The fighting began at noon. I was given messages to carry: the very first was to Pearse and Connolly, who were occupying the Post Office.

The GPO was a very grand building in Sackville Street. Across the street was Nelson's Pillar, sign of British domination. (I was so glad when they blew that pillar up in the 1960s. I never thought it would go in my lifetime!) I took my dispatch to the leaders of the Rebellion, and I must say they didn't look like the heroes they really were. Connolly was a little fat man with a great big moustache; Pearse was wall-eyed, God bless the mark! I had met him before at a ceilidh. He was a lovely, handsome man, and was known then as the leader of the movement...

The men of my family and my husband were all in Jacob's biscuit factory in Wexford Street: Jacob's Garrison we called it. The

Volunteers had taken it and defended it all the week.

You must remember, though, that some half of the family were off to fight for the British in the First World War. Jim Behan, the brother of my second husband, was killed in the front line on the Somme. His name is on the Arches to the Fallen at St Stephen's Green. My son Seamus is called after him. Jack Furlong's brother Harry was in the British Army, too. Every house had a son serving in the British Army, so there were many against the Rebellion. In some ways Dublin had done well out of the war. The war meant money for those who might not have had work without it, and the Irish had always supplied the British Army's horses.

So there was no mass support for us. A crowd gathered around Jacob's, shouting, 'If you want to fight, go to France!' Dublin was divided over the Rebellion. One friend of mine, Mrs Slater, lost three sons in it – and she wasn't a rebel at all.

But some of the men who'd joined the British Army were for us, and gave information about what their plans were. It was from one of them that we learned that the British planned to shell the buildings we had taken. No one had thought that the British would destroy their own property – that was why the plan was to take and occupy large buildings, rather than fight in the streets. Our aim was always to defend, rather than attack.

Down at St Stephen's Green the great Countess Markievicz was showing that women can hold their ground too. She was a member of the Irish Citizen Army – the armed section of the trade unions – although she was one of the upper classes. She was born a Gore-Booth, and became the greatest horsewoman in Ireland. She learned her courage on the hunting field, going over the very wildest fences with the men trotting after. Don't forget that they rode side-saddle in those days.

Anyway, as soon as the Rebellion started she was out there in her uniform – which consisted of an immense floppy hat and a green tunic and skirt. It was supposed to be based on the uniform of the Boers when they fought the British in South Africa. She started to dig a hole in St Stephens' Green, to defend it against assault by the Brits.

Now, although there was all this fighting going on, many people were trying their best to ignore it and go on working as usual. Near her dug-out were some men working on scaffolding, and they started to jeer at this mad woman in uniform digging a hole in the middle of a park. In the end she couldn't stand it any longer, and loosed off at them with her pistol, which she carried with her. They didn't stay at work after that.

...The British crushed our Rebellion easily enough – after all, they had thirty thousand to our six hundred. They even brought a gunboat up the River Liffey and beat the heart out of the city. It was a sad sight to see the captured rebels, some led in chains down to the boats bound for the prison camps in England. The others – our leaders – well, they were for something else. A death party. Most of them could not believe that brave men taken in battle would be shot like mad dogs, but they were, and even though their bodies were burned in quicklime, Ireland forever held their graves.

Brian Behan: Mother of All the Behans, pp. 38-40; 42-3.

THE GENERAL POST OFFICE

When the Rising came, it came unknown to me anyway. I had a job in the convent in Eccles Street; and at the time of the Easter Holidays, I went out to lodgings to have quiet and to write my thesis for the MA. That's what I was doing on Easter Monday when a girl ran into the house shouting out that the GPO had been seized by the Volunteers as well as other places in the city; and that the Rising was on. I didn't believe the story at first, but it was confirmed to me, and I told myself that I would have to go out, and see how it was.

I walked down to O'Connell Street, nobody was prohibited yet, and I reached the GPO without any difficulty. A Volunteer was standing guard at the door; I asked him to let me in, that I wanted to speak with Patrick Pearse – the only person I knew in the place, from having taught in Saint Ita's [the Irish-speaking school set up by Pearse]. I was taken to him, he listened to me quietly and courteously and I did a very bold thing, which makes me shiver when I think of it today. I informed him that I didn't agree with what they had done, that we had no hope in my opinion; that we would be defeated – and because of that it was not right to take part in the fight – but if there was to be a fight that I wanted to be present ... Pearse's outlook was: he understood that every Irish person (both men and women) could serve Ireland and he wouldn't wish to come between anyone and that privilege. He answered that he would send me up to the kitchen, where I could attend to the Volunteers. I was completely satisfied and I was sent up. The kitchen was up stairs and there was a big room beside it, which I think was a dining room for the post office people. I was introduced to Desmond Fitzgerald who was in charge of the place. I had never seen him before that, although I knew his wife well. Desmond had spent six months in prison and he had come out a short time before that. I got to know him on Easter Monday and we spent the week working together in the kitchen...

Neither of us were too knowledgeable about cooking affairs or on providing food, but there was a girl there who had come across from

Liverpool to be in the Rising and she was very experienced at that type of work. Peggy Downey was her name. She examined and estimated the food that the Volunteers had collected and she estimated that the food would last three or four weeks if we were very careful about it. Desmond told that to Pearse and Pearse said: 'Take all the care in the world about it then, for nobody knows how long it will be needed.'

The boys would come down from the roof of the building and from the big hall to get meals. We had three prisoners also – two officers and a soldier I think – and there was a priest there also who was brought in to hear confessions if there was anybody hurt: Father Flanagan of the Pro-Cathedral.

The week went on then. I wouldn't go down to the hall and I didn't know anything except what Desmond told me. The front of the building was burning from Thursday but we didn't take notice of it; we were at the back of the building and a good distance from the fire. On Friday morning, I think, we were told that the Volunteers were to leave the place and we would have to take the wounded people to Jervis Street hospital. We went down to the hall – the girls who were working down below were sent home before that and we were talking to the boys and collecting messages from them for their people.

Later in the evening – around six or seven I think – everything was ready. The Volunteers went out and we ourselves hit the road ... We were told to bail out from the back of the house, out to a little yard, over a wall and in through houses in Henry Street which the Volunteers had broken gaps in, so that we would be able to reach Jervis Street without going out into Henry Street, where shooting was continuing.

I would say there were between sixteen and twenty of us. Desmond Fitzgerald and the priest were guiding us; a boy who was training to be a doctor and six or seven injured boys, one person who had a bullet in his body and couldn't walk – others who had hurt an eye or a hand, boys who were added to our numbers to help them and to carry the wounded man and a small number of girls – that was what was left when the majority was sent home on Thursday.

Louise Gavan Duffy: 'In San GPO: Cumann na mBan', (ed.) F X Martin: *1916 and University College Dublin*, pp. 91-5, (translated by Brendan Ó Fiach).

THE FOUR COURTS

On Easter Sunday morning, 23 April, 1916, on our way home from early Mass, my sister Aine and myself heard a newsboy shouting 'Stop Press!' and to our amazement learned of Eoin MacNeill's order countermanding the Sunday parade. We naturally felt confused when we read the parade was off. Later Mrs Joe McGuinness who was a Lieutenant in the First Battalion, called at my address ... saying that the arrangements for Sunday were off but that I was to 'stand to' and await further orders.

At about 8 pm we went in search of news to the Keating Branch of the Gaelic League at North Frederick Street. Here we met some of the Volunteers who, like ourselves, were eagerly seeking information. No one seemed to know anything definite and after a while we returned home. Everybody seemed to be on edge and as much at sea as ourselves; the atmosphere was quite abnormal.

Early on Monday morning a despatch was brought to my digs from Mrs McGuinness, stating that Cumann na mBan were to report for duty at Palmerstone Place in vicinity of the Black Church and the Broadstone at 12 noon. I got instructions to collect some of our members on the way with full kit as was previously arranged...

We remained in this area all day and were very disappointed at getting no work to do. The Volunteers at this stage were in, or had taken possession of, the posts and outposts allotted to the different battalions and already firing was heard. This was the first definite indication that the fight was on. Nobody had ever told me that there was to be a Rising, but I was convinced from the general preparations and activities that one was to take place. Intermittent firing went on during the day and we still had no word of what was happening. At about 6 pm we got orders which were brought by a dispatch-rider on a bicycle that we were to go home, as our services would not be required. We had no alternative but to obey the orders.

On our way home we were amused by a crowd of women fitting on fancy boots and doling out loot to one another at the top of North Great George's Street. Emily Elliott accompanied me to Mrs Cleary's where I was staying and we decided to volunteer at the General Post Office for work in any capacity if the Volunteers had sufficient nurses, as we were given to understand they had. When we arrived at the General Post Office and interviewed the sentry, he told us they had enough staff and our services would not be required. He suggested we should report for duty to an outpost on the opposite side of O'Connell Street, which was occupied by the Volunteers. This we did and the Volunteers in Reis's Chambers gave us a hearty *Céad Míle Fáilte*. We were soon busy helping in our small way. In this building was a wireless school and the Volunteers were endeavouring to establish communications with the outside world, particularly with America ... There was no food or facilities for cooking in the building. We awaited daylight on Tuesday morning to go across to the General Post Office for rations for the men. With great difficulty we crossed O'Connell Street, which was a mass of barbed wire and barricades.

However, we were admitted after a minute interrogation. We explained our mission and were escorted to the food controller. Here the late Desmond Fitzgerald was in charge ... At first he was reluctant to comply with our request but we were so persistent that he ultimately yielded to our appeal.

After the meal and when we had tidied up, we decided to look up Emily Elliott's sister, Eilis. We went back to their digs and found her. On the way we delivered two dispatches ... We returned to Reis's Chambers and on our arrival word came that members of Cumann na mBan were required at the Four Courts outpost. We volunteered, said 'Slan Libh!' to our friends and left O'Connell Street for the Four Court's garrison.

When we reached the Four Courts, after wending our way through high, narrow streets to avoid stray bullets, we were told to report to the Father Mathew Hall, Church Street, which had been handed over for a first-aid station to Commandant Daly by the Capuchin Fathers ...

Each member of Cumann na mBan was supplied with a white armlet and consequently became a member of the hospital staff. We realised that we were officially attached to a first aid unit. We were allotted our duties by the senior members of our branch. The Volunteers supplied the hospital with plenty of food including ham, tomatoes, tea and sugar and, I think, milk. I there sampled tomatoes and sugarless tea for the first time in my life. We helped in the kitchen for the first few days but members qualified in first-aid were then transferred to the Hall which had now been fitted up with improvised stretcher beds which had been commandeered. These were ranged in such a way as to avoid stray bullets that might penetrate through the windows.

For the first few days of the fighting, wounds treated were of a minor nature but as time went on the number of more seriously wounded patients increased and we carried them on stretchers into the hall and dressed their wounds. This work and that of carrying food to the men at the numerous barricades in Church Street, continued up to Friday. One such barricade erected beside the church had a cab in the centre and, when going to the Four Courts, it was necessary to go through the doors ...

On Thursday morning we visited the members of Cumann na mBan at the Four Courts ... Commandant Daly had been in and out of the hall several times during the week and spoke very highly of the men of the First Battalion. I remember taking off his boots and socks on Wednesday, bathing his feet and giving him fresh socks with plenty of boric powder. He said he felt very comfortable after it. He spoke very highly of the Volunteers and their comrades in arms and of the wonderful assistance given by our organisation ...

The firing was heavy on Saturday. The noise of rifle fire was deafening. Soon we learned that the military were closing in on the outskirts of our area and that our dear comrades were vacating their outposts and retreating to their headquarters in the Four Courts ... Towards nightfall there came a lull and the military passed along the street towards the Four Courts where by this time all Volunteers, who had manned the outposts and barricades, had taken refuge. It was then decided that all the patients whose wounds were of a serious nature should be removed to Richmond Hospital before any raiding or investigation took place. We were under the stretchers once more and managed to get the hall cleared in a short period ... When we returned to the Father Mathew Hall it was now deserted. All our staff and friends had now left the building except Father Augustine and Brother Pacificus. Now we were faced with the problem, 'Where to go or what to do'. There were only four of us left – the Elliott sisters, Kathleen Kenny and myself. Father Augustine was most sympathetic and said we could not be turned out at that hour – it must have been now 11 pm. He ... suggested we rest in the church in a small room beside the high altar. Brother Pacificus fitted up the place with some bedding which he brought in from the vacated hospital. He also heated the room with an electric fire. We gladly accepted this dear friend's hospitality ... Father Augustine told us to leave in the morning when the Angelus bell rang and before the church doors should be opened, to attend the early mass and then mingle with the congregation when leaving so that we could quietly get away. As far as I can remember we did not sleep, as the noise outside was still deafening. There was intermittent firing and we had fears as to what was happening or about to happen to our comrades.

Brother Pacificus knocked at the door of our room before the appointed time and left us a tray with tea, bread and butter. This came as a great surprise and was very welcome as we had not tasted food for a long time. We eventually took up our positions in the church and were surprised to see some of our Volunteer friends also in attendance. They probably had been given shelter too.

We carried out Father Augustine's instructions and by degrees mingled with the congregation. When we came out of the church there were crowds outside, people who had come in search of their dear ones or to make enquiries about them. This was a great help to us in moving off. We wended our way for home back through the narrow streets. Every street corner was now lined with armed British tommies and after zigzagging from one street to another in order to avoid the soldiers, we reached North Frederick Street in the evening, having passed another day without food – except the breakfast we got in the morning from Brother Pacificus. Here we met two members of the Keating Branch who escorted us to the friendly restaurant of the Misses Molloy where we were treated to tea. They were more than kind and sympathetic. We then made our way to Fleming's Hotel, Gardiner's Place, where we met Mrs McGuinness and Miss McMahon, our secretary. We were welcomed back, and we told our experiences during the week and also heard the   stories of other members of Cumann na mBan.

Eilis Bean Uí Chonail: 'A Cumann na mBan Recalls Easter Week', *The Capuchin Annual* 1966, pp. 271-8

THE IRISH CITIZEN ARMY
The experience of the women members of the Irish Citizen Army differed from that of their counterparts in Cumann na mBan. Male and female members of the Citizen Army assembled together at Liberty Hall on the Easter Monday before marching off to carry out their already allotted tasks. The shortage of manpower meant that those women who wished to were able to undertake a military role.

STEPHEN'S GREEN
I am afraid I can only give you a little account of those who were enrolled like me in the Irish Citizen Army, and those who were with me or whom I met during the week. Some were members of Cumann na mBan, and others just women who were ready to die for Ireland.

My activities were confined to a very limited area. I was mobilised for Liberty Hall and was sent from there via the City Hall, to Stephen's Green, where I remained.

On Easter Monday there was a great hosting of disciplined and armed men and women at Liberty Hall. Padraig Pearse and James Connolly addressed us and told us that from now on the Volunteers and the ICA were not two forces, but two wings of the Irish Republican Army.

There were a considerable number of ICA women. These were absolutely on the same footing as the men. They took part in all marches, and even in the manoeuvres that lasted all night. Moreover, Connolly made it quite clear to us that unless we women took our share in the drudgery of training and preparing, we should not be allowed to take any share at all in the fight. You may judge how fit we were when I tell you that sixteen miles was the length of the average route march.

Connolly had appointed two staff officers – Commandant Mallin and myself. I held a commission, giving me the rank of Staff Lieutenant. I was accepted by Tom Clarke and the members of the Provisional Government as the second of Connolly's 'ghosts'. Ghosts was the name we gave to those who stood secretly behind the leaders, and who were entrusted with enough of the plans of the Rising to enable them to carry on that leader's work should anything happen to himself. Commandant Mallin was over me and next in command to Connolly. Dr Kathleen Lynn was our medical officer, holding the rank of Captain.

We watched the little bodies of men and women march off – Pearse and Connolly to the GPO, Sean Connolly to the City Hall. I went with the Doctor in her car. We carried a huge store of first-aid necessities and drove off through the quiet, dusty streets and across the river, reaching the City Hall just at the very moment Commandant Sean Connolly and his little troop of men and women swung round the corner and he raised his gun and shot the policeman who barred the way. A wild excitement ensued, people running from every side to see what was up. The Doctor got out, and I remember Mrs Barrett – sister of Sean Connolly – and others helping to carry in the Doctor's bundle. I did not meet Dr Lynn again till my release, when her car met me, and she welcomed me to her house where she cared for me and fed me up and looked after me till I had recovered from the evil effects of the English prison system.

When I reported with the car to Commandant Mallin in Stephen's Green he told me that he must keep me. He said that, owing to MacNeill's call-off of the Volunteers, a lot of the men who should have been under him had had to be distributed round other posts and that few of those left him were trained to shoot, so I must stay and be ready to take up the work of a sniper. He took me round the Green and showed me how the barricading of the gates and digging trenches had begun, and left me in charge of this work while he went to superintend the erection of barricades in the street and arrange other work. About two hours later he definitely promoted me to be his second-in-command. This work was very exciting when the fighting began. I continued to go round and round the Green, reporting back if anything was wanted or tackling any sniper who was particularly objectionable.

Madeleine ffrench-Mullen was in charge of the Red Cross and the commissariart in the Green. Some of the girls had revolvers and with these they sallied forth and held up bread-vans.

This was necessary, because the first prisoner we took was a

British officer, and Commandant Mallin treated him as such. He took his parole as 'an officer and a gentleman' not to escape and he left him at large in the Green before the gates were shut. This English gentleman walked around and found out all he could and then 'bunked.'

We had a couple of sick men and prisoners in the band-stand, the Red Cross flag flying to protect them. The English in the Shelbourne turned a machine-gun on to them. A big group of our girls were attending to the sick, making tea for the prisoners, or resting themselves. I never saw anything like their courage. Madeleine ffrench-Mullen brought them, with the sick and the prisoners, out and into a safer place. It was all done slowly and in perfect order. More than one girl said to me: 'What is there to be afraid of? Won't I go straight to heaven if I die for Ireland.' However it was, they came out unscathed from under a shower of shrapnel.

On Tuesday we began to be short of food. There were no bread carts on the streets. We retired into the College of Surgeons that evening and were joined by some of our men, who had been in other places, and by quite a large squad of Volunteers, and with this increase in our numbers the problem of food became very serious.

Nellie Gifford was put in charge of one large class-room with a big grate; but alas! there was nothing to cook. When we were all starving she produced a quantity of oatmeal from somewhere and made pot after potful of the most delicious porridge, which kept us going. But, all the same, on Tuesday and Wednesday we absolutely starved. There seemed to be no bread in the town.

Later on Mary Hyland was given charge of a little kitchen somewhere down through the houses, near where the Eithne Workroom now is.

We had only one woman casualty – Margaret Skinnider. She, like myself, was in uniform and carried an army rifle. She had enlisted as a private in the ICA. She was one of a party who went out to set fire to a house just behind Russell's Hotel. The English opened fire on them from the ground floor of a house just opposite. Poor Freddy Ryan was killed and Margaret was very badly wounded. She owes her life to William Partridge. He carried her away under fire and back to the College.

God rest his noble soul! Brilliant orator and labour leader, comrade and friend of Connolly's, he was content to serve as a private in the ICA. He was never strong and the privations he suffered in an English jail left him a dying man.

Margaret's only regret was her bad luck in being disabled so early in the day, though she must have suffered terribly; but the end was nearer than we thought, for it was only a few days later that we had her carried over to Vincent's Hospital, so that she would not fall wounded into the hands of the English.

The memory of Easter Week with its heroic dead is sacred to us who survived. Many of us could almost wish we had died in the moment of ecstasy when, with the Tricolour over our heads we went out and proclaimed the Irish Republic and with guns in our hands tried to establish it. We failed, but not until we had seen regiment after regiment run from our few guns. Our effort will inspire the people who come after us and will give them hope and courage. If we failed to win, so did the English. They slaughtered and imprisoned, only to rouse the nation to a passion of love and loyalty – loyalty to Ireland and hatred of foreign rule. Once they see clearly that the English rule us still, only with a new personnel of traitors and new uniforms, they will finish the work begun by the men and women of Easter Week.

> Constance de Markievicz: *Cumann na nBan*,
> Vol. II No. 10, Easter 1926

ANOTHER MEMORY OF STEPHEN'S GREEN

Singing 'Soldiers are we whose lives are pledged to Ireland', we had withdrawn from St Stephen's Green into the College of Surgeons. Only one of our men had been killed. Yet this was a retreat, and we knew it. If only we had had enough men to take possession of the Shelbourne Hotel, we need not have yielded the Green. As it was, we wasted no time in mourning, but went to work at once to make ourselves ready for a siege that might last no one knew how long ...

On Wednesday there was little despatch-bearing to do, so I stood around watching the men up there at work. The Countess realized my impatience to be doing my bit, also my hesitation at putting myself forward without permission. Without saying anything to me, she went to Commandant Mallin and told him she thought I could be of use under the roof. He gave his permission at once, and she brought me the answer.

Madam had had a fine uniform of green moleskin made for me. With her usual generosity, she had mine made of better material than her own. It consisted of knee-breeches, belted coat, and puttees. I slipped into this uniform, climbed up astride the rafters, and was assigned a loophole through which to shoot. It was dark there, full of smoke and the din of firing, but it was good to be in action. I could look across the tops of trees and see the British soldiers on the roof of the Shelbourne. I could also hear their shot hailing against the roof and wall of our fortress, for in truth this building was just that. More than once I saw the man I aimed at fall.

Every shot we fired was a declaration to the world that Ireland, a small country but large in our hearts, was demanding her independence. We knew that all over Dublin, perhaps by this time all over Ireland, other groups like ours were filled with the same intensity, the same determination, to make the Irish Republic, no matter how short-lived, a reality of which history would have to take account...

Whenever I was called down to carry a despatch, I took off my uniform, put on my grey dress and hat, and went out the side door of the college with my message. As soon as I returned, I slipped back into my uniform and joined the firing-squad...

I was up-stairs, studying a map of our surroundings and trying to find a way by which we could dislodge the soldiers from the roof of the Hotel Shelbourne. When Commandant Mallin came in, I asked him if he would let me go out with one man and try to throw a bomb attached to an eight-second fuse through the hotel window. I knew there was a bow-window on the side farthest from us, which was not likely to be guarded. We could use our bicycles and get away before the bomb exploded – that is, if we were quick enough. At any rate, it was worth trying, whatever the cost.

Commandant Mallin agreed the plan was a good one, but much too dangerous. I pointed out to him that it had been my speed which had saved me so far from machine-gun fire on the hotel roof. It was not that the British were doing us any real harm in the college, but it was high time to take the aggressive, for success would hearten the men in other 'forts' who were not having as safe a time of it. He finally agreed, though not at all willingly, for he did not want to let a woman run this sort of risk. My answer to that argument was that we had the same right to risk our lives as the men; that in the Constitution of the Irish Republic, women were on an equality with men. For the first time in history, indeed, a Constitution had been written that incorporated the principle of equal suffrage. But the Commandant told me there was another task to be accomplished before the hotel could be bombed. That was to cut off the retreat of a British force which had planted a machine-gun on the flat roof of University Church ... This church, close at hand, had been occupied by the British, and was cutting us off from another command with whom it was necessary to keep in communication. In order to cut off the retreat of these soldiers, it would be necessary to burn two buildings. I asked the commandant to let me help in this undertaking. He consented, and gave me four men to help fire one building, while another party went out to fire the other. It meant a great deal to me that he should trust me with this piece of work, and I felt elated. While I changed once more into my uniform, for the work of war can only be done by those who wear its dress, I could still hear them singing...

It took only a few moments to reach the building we were to set afire. Councillor Partridge smashed the glass door in the front of a shop that occupied the ground floor. He did it with the butt of his rifle and a flash followed. It had been discharged! I rushed past him into the doorway of the shop, calling to the others to come on. Behind me came the sound of a volley, and I fell. It was as I had on the instant divined. That flash had revealed us to the enemy.

'It's all over,' I muttered, as I felt myself falling. But a moment later, when I knew I was not dead, I was sure I should pull through. Before another volley could be fired, Mr Partridge lifted and carried me into the street ...

They laid me on a large table and cut away the coat of my fine, new uniform. I cried over that. Then they found I had been shot in three places, my right side under the arm, my right arm, and in the back on my right side. Had I not turned as I went through that shop-door to call the others, I would have got all three bullets in my back and lungs and surely been done for.

Margaret Skinnider: *Doing My Bit for Ireland*, pp. 132-48

DUBLIN CASTLE

The Rising was called off but the Citizen Army took no notice of that ... It was decided to go out if we only went out by ourselves – the Citizen Army. So on Easter Monday we assembled outside Liberty Hall, down there in Beresford Place, for the march off, the attack on the GPO. Most of the Volunteers were to attack there. Well, our party of the Citizen Army, under Connolly's supreme command of course, we were to start off at 12 o'clock – 12 o'clock was the time exactly, but 5 minutes before that or less, my little party under a young captain called Sean Connolly – no relation of James Connolly at all – he was a young captain, a young actor that I knew very well – we started off to attack Dublin Castle. That was our orders. The girls were all served with revolvers, I had my own at the time. And we started off, up King's Street, just a little ahead of the others start off. Well, when we came to Dublin Castle gate, Connolly led us round to the gate and the sentry, the British sentry who was inside in his box saw us, surprised and I suppose electrified, he rushed forward and he banged the gates in our faces just in the nick of time, to shut us out. So, Sean Connolly, who had been a clerk in the City Hall, which is practically part of Dublin Castle, he knew the ropes and got a little side gate, a tiny side gate there, open ... there was no difficulty about us rushing in, girls and men together, into the City Hall and I and some of the girls went up to the very top, looking for the kitchen, which we wanted to arrive at, in order to take care of the Commissariat for the men and a place for the wounded, if any. So we established ourselves in one of the very top rooms in the City Hall ... and then the cross-firing continued, very rapidly.

Sean Connolly asked me to go over to the GPO to ask for re-inforcements and I went out and down Dame Street and there I met Frank Sheehy Skeffington ... very agitated and perturbed looking, but quite calm. He was walking in the middle of the road, taking no notice of the bullets ... he was very brave, he was a pacifist – he always said 'I am ready to die for Ireland but I will not kill for Ireland.' That was his slogan. So I got over to the GPO and asked, made my request to James Connolly who told me to tell Sean that he'ld send men as soon as he could. So I went back again and soon after that Sean Connolly was hit. He was hit somewhere in the body, hit very badly ... he wasn't able to speak. So I dispatched one of our girls up to Stephen's Green where Dr Kathleen Lynn was with Michael Mallin – she was Medical Officer of the Citizen Army and she came down and went up and she said 'I'm afraid he's going', and in a few minutes he did go. I knelt beside him, said a few prayers into his ear, and his little brother, a younger brother about fifteen, was crying bitterly, oh so bitterly, by his side. So Sean passed, a very sad and very moving death.

Fighting continued all day until lateish in the evening when there was a crashing...downstairs and a loud voice said 'Surrender in the King's name' so we went downstairs and we had a wounded boy and the bullets were flying and the plaster from the ceiling, a very ornate plaster ceiling, was crashing down on the floor and I put this boy into a porter's chair, a hooded chair, I pushed him up against a pillar and he asked me to hold his hand, which I did. Then Dr Lynn answered the challenger and said 'We surrender', after some minutes. So we were taken out of the back window there, into the Castle yard and bought into Ship Street barracks, all of us, men and women, that were taken. And there we were for a couple of days, very uncomfortable, no beds, nothing to lie on, with single blankets, but there we stayed until we were moved to Kilmainham. I was with the girls, brought up into one of the upper galleries where some of the men were, including James Connolly. But every morning we heard shots in the yard below and there was something sinister about them, we knew the men were being shot. Which was the truth, they were. So that was a terrible experience, and that went on...a week or so, maybe more. We were then removed to Mountjoy prison.

Helena Moloney: radio interview,
published by Ceiruiní Claddaigh, 1966

CHAPTER 5

After the Rising

TAKING OUR PLACE
In reading of Ireland's glorious past we find the women taking their rightful place in Arts, Literature, Legislation, and even in the making of War.

The Irish woman of today is debarred from entering on many a sphere which she would desire.

Are we competent to take our proper place in the New Ireland which is dawning for us?

Let us see to it that we be worthy successors of Brigid, Maeb and Grainne Maol.

> Áine Ceannt: Foreword to Crissie M. Doyle
> (C. Máire Ní Dubgaill): *Women in Ancient and Modern Ireland*.

A PRISONER'S RETURN
One morning, in the coldness before dawn, the streets of Dublin heard the patter of running feet. Somehow, from the port of Dunleary miles away, word had filtered through that the prisoners taken in the Rising and lodged in English pri-sons had been landed: landed at that early hour and without warning, to prevent a reception of any kind. But there was going to be a reception. Newsboys, young men, sympathis-ers of every kind, running on foot brought the news to Dublin. The citizens were trooping to Dunleary on foot. There were no cars at that hour of the morning, no railway trains, and only a few people had autos. But the people were there. They formed a cheering procession and escorted the released prisoners into Dublin. The news spread; folk threw up their windows, flags appeared, from house to house the occupants tumbled into the street, eager for news, eager for a sight of the returned heroes. De Valera was there.

'Where is the Countess Markievicz?' was the cry. 'We want the Countess!'

'She is not coming into Dublin till tomorrow. There will be a real reception for the Countess. It takes a day to prepare it. She is the people's Countess, and we will give a proper welcome to her!'

Next day, toward evening, the Countess entered Dublin in the midst of a long procession, with banner after banner and brass band after brass band; with riders on horseback; with running boys waving branches; with lumbering floats drawn by big slow-footed good-natured Clydesdale horses; with trade-guilds carrying emblems; with public notabilities in uniform; with ragged urchins from the slums – a glad and multitudinous company laughing, shouting, and singing.

Upon a float piled high with flowers and greenery the Countess stood, very fair to look on, radiant and slender. Towering beside her was a large Sinn Féin flag: green and orange and white. From a window I could see the River Liffey, curving between its wharves and tall narrow-fronted houses, spanned by bridge upon bridge till lost in the distance. When the Countess crossed the bridge nearest to me, every bridge behind her was a-toss with red flags, and the people were singing *The International*. I had a window over a baker's shop. The woman of the shop knew me. She knew boys who had attended my classes, my talks on Irish history. She said to me: 'I want to tell you there wasn't one of the boys that didn't fight in the Rising.'

The woman was pale and thin. She had seen too little of the sunlight. The shop was a poor one, scantily furnished: flies buzzed in it. The woman had not given herself a holiday to join in the procession, yet she was more than part of it. She was one of those who made that triumphant pageant possible. For half a lifetime she had spent her few free hours in work for the Irish cause. She had given with both hands out of her meagre possessions, taking no thought for the morrow. Her man had been in the fighting though he had to rise from a sick-bed to shoulder his rifle. He was free now of the sick-bed and the burden of life.

She did not think that she had done anything noteworthy. She did not think of herself at all.

Ella Young: *Flowering Dusk*, pp. 132-4

EQUALITY FOR IRISH WOMEN?

In April 1917, one year after the Rising, an informal group, calling themselves the 'Conference of Women Delegates', began to meet. Their first act was to write to Sinn Féin, demanding an equality of status for women within the organisation.

Dear Sir

At a meeting held on Monday 30 July at 44 Oakley Road, Mrs Ceannt in the Chair, I was instructed to write to you concerning the important question of the adequate representation of women on your Executive Council. As you know, the women of Ireland have at present only one representative, namely Countess Plunkett.

Seeing that you are enlarging your Council to include six members of the Irish Nation League elected by that body, and also six prisoners to be elected by the prisoners, the time seems opportune to include also six women, elected by women.

The claim of women to be represented is based mainly on the Republican Proclamation of Easter Week, 1916, which of course, you are determined to uphold:

'The Irish Republic is entitled to, and hereby claims the allegiance of every Irishman and Irishwoman. The Republic guarantees religious and civil liberty, equal rights and equal opportunities to all its citizens.'

The claim is also based on the risks women took, equally with the men, to have the Irish Republic established, on the necessity of having their organised cooperation in the further struggle to free Ireland and the advantage of having their ideas on many social problems likely to arise in the near future.

The names I am to put forward are:

Mrs Clarke, Mrs Ceannt, Dr Lynn, Mrs Wyse-Power, Miss Moloney, Mrs Ginnell.

Awaiting the pleasure of your reply,

I remain, dear sir,

Yours faithfully,

Alice Ginnell, Hon. Sec. Pro. Tem.

Minutes of Conference of Women Delegates, 1 August 1917: *Sheehy-Skeffington Papers* MS 21,194. National Library of Ireland

SINN FEIN CONVENTION 1917

Resolution of League of Women Delegates, adopted by Sinn Féin at its Convention of 1917:

Whereas, according to the Republican Proclamation which guarantees 'religious and civil liberty, equal rights and equal opportunities to all its citizens', women are equally eligible with men as members of branches, members of the governing body and officers of both local and governing bodies, be it resolved: that the equality of men and women in this organisation be emphasised in all speeches and leaflets.

Dr Kathleen Lynn:

Women and men are complements one of the other . . . .as a whole I think that women are honster [sic] than men and work straight for their end without being held back by personal considerations. We see all around us a system rotten with corruption and intrigue. If women have their place it will be much easier to keep it honest and open and straight. There would have been no Easter Week had it not been for the women who urged the men to take action boldly. We have no doubt now that Easter Week saved Ireland ... We are inexperienced, different and timid, we ask the men with centuries of experience to give us a little help and encouragement at the start, so as to give us a fair share in the great work before us (Applause).

Mrs Jenny Wyse-Power:
I second the resolution. The resolution as it stands does not mean more than that when they mention the men of Ireland they should also include the women of Ireland. I think we are all clearly satisfied that the same status must be given to women as to men in Ireland. I do not agree with what Dr Lynn said, that only for the women of Ireland you would have no Easter Week. The women cheered and encouraged the fighting, but the men went out and fought.

Chair (Arthur Griffith):
I ask the delegates to pass this without any further discussion. From the day we founded Sinn Féin we made no discrimination as to sex for any office in the organisation ... It must be made clear that women are just as eligible as men for any position in the country.
(Editor: the word 'all' in the resolution was removed as a misprint and the resolution was then carried, following speeches for the amendment by Father O'Flanagan and Sean T. O'Kelly.)

Sinn Féin Convention Report MS 21,523. National Library of Ireland

FEMINIST REACTION TO THE SINN FEIN CONVENTION

We offer our hearty congratulations to the promoters and spokesmen of the Sinn Féin Convention for the broad statesmanship and the public spirit they have displayed in endorsing and embodying in the new Constitution, in the most unequivocal terms, the democratic principle of the complete equality of men and women in Ireland ... The outstanding feature in the discussion on the new Constitution of Sinn Féin was the fine spirited speech of Dr Kathleen Lynn in support of the motion on the agenda with reference to women's equality. The motion was seconded by Mrs Wyse-Power and warmly supported by Councillor Sean T O'Kelly, who pointed out that in endorsing this principle Irishmen were only returning to the traditions of Gaelic Ireland and rejecting the teaching of an alien civilization; and any

Irishman who could oppose women's claim for equality would be acting in an unIrish spirit. The motion was carried unanimously by the Convention. At an earlier stage in the discussion, one of the women delegates, Miss Rosamund Jacob, of Waterford, raised an important point as to how Sinn Féin would secure the views of women with reference to the Constituent Assembly it proposed to set up, since under existing machinery Irishwomen did not possess the franchise. The Chairman replied that any machinery set up to secure the representation of the view of the whole people of Ireland would be adjusted to include the women of the country. It was regrettable to notice so few women delegates, an inequality which we strongly hope to see rectified on the occasion of future Conventions.

The splendid recognition of women's equality with men by the Sinn Féin Convention is a triumphant vindication of the sound political wisdom of the Irish militants in placing suffrage first, especially during the trying period of the European War, and perhaps the still more trying period since the rebellion.

Irish Citizen, November 1917

CUMANN NA D'TEACHTAIRE
The League of Women Delegates adopted the Irish name Cumann na d'Teachtaire and drew up a constitution with the following aims:

To safeguard the political rights of Irishwomen.

To ensure adequate representation for them in the Republican Government.

To urge and facilitate the appointment of women to Public Boards throughout the country.

To educate Irishwomen in the rights and duties of citizenship.

Minutes of Cumann na d'Teachtaire, 16 October 1917:
Sheehy-Skeffington Papers MS 21,194. National Library of Ireland

CUMANN NA mBAN CONVENTION 1917
At the Cumann na mBan Convention of 1917 significant changes were made to the policies of the organisation as nationalist women continued to assert their claims to political equality.

Policy for 1917-1918
1. To continue collecting for the 'Defence of Ireland' Fund and any other fund to be devoted to the arming and equipping of the men and women of Ireland.

2. To assist in the movement to secure representation of Ireland at the Peace Conference by the election of Republican candidates, etc.

3. To follow the policy of the Republican Proclamation by seeing that women take up their proper position in the life of the nation.

Members of Cumann na mBan should participate in the public life of their locality and assert their right as citizens to take part in the nominations of candidates for parliamentary and local elections.

Branches should take steps to educate women by means of lectures, literature, debates and classes in the conduct of public affairs, so that they might be acquainted with the correct forms of procedure to be followed at all meetings in which they take part and may be fitted to occupy public positions.

Cumann na nBan Convention Report, 1917.
National Library of Ireland

1918 ELECTION
In 1918 British and Irish women over the age of 30 were given the right to vote and to stand for election to parliament. Women were singled out as an important new group of voters whose support was vital to the future of the country.

AN APPEAL TO THE WOMEN OF IRELAND
Not without reason did the old time poets in Eirinn call the country they loved by a woman's name. To them Ireland, for whose liberation they strove so heroically was a mystical woman in captivity, at the mercy of a brutal enemy. Their devotion to Dark Rosaleen and their love of her were both boundless because in woman the ancient Gael saw the great glory of his race, the sure promise that the sacred tradition of the Gaelic people would be carried into the unnumbered generations of the future.

To the same bearers of the spiritual heritage of the mystical Rosaleen this appeal is today directed. Our enemies will call it a political appeal – an appeal by factionists. But it is no other then the cry of Sarsfield's wearied troops to the valiant women of Limerick and it is no less honourable and urgent. The women of Ireland have for seven centuries preserved to the Gael the ideal of independence ... In the days of the Land League the women were as valiant champions of the dispossessed race as the farmers themselves. And today the voices of Sarsfield and Tone and Emmet and Mitchell and Parnell and Pearse – the grateful voices of the dead cry to the women of Ireland to stand by their tortured sister Rosaleen ...

You can save Ireland by voting as Mrs Pearse will vote ... The choice is largely with the women of Ireland. They can win for us the ancient ideal of our people. All their history, all their idealism, all their self-interest, all their commonsense must prove to them that Sinn Féin is the one party meriting their support, that it is the only party worthy of the past; representing the heroic feeling of the present; having in it any hope for the future of the People of Ireland.

We appeal to the women voters all over Ireland to vote with Sinn Féin, because the physical safety of the race depends upon our immediate freedom; because Sinn Féin carries on the tradition of independence which, thanks to the Gaelic Mother, still lives in Ireland; because in every generation Irish women have played a noble part in the struggle for freedom; because finally as in the past, so in the future the womenfolk of the Gael shall have a high place in the Councils of a freed Gaelic nation.

Sinn Féin: *An Appeal to the Women of Ireland*, 1918.
National Library of Ireland.

THE PRESENT DUTY OF IRISHWOMEN
Cumann na mBan also issued a leaflet, urging women to support Sinn Féin in the election.

Sinn Féin must sweep Ireland at the General Election if our country is to be freed in our time. You can help to free her by securing your vote and using it in the right way. You can find out if you are entitled to a vote, and if so, how to set about getting it, from the local Cumann na mBan branch (or if there is none in your district, from the local Sinn Féin Club).

DON'T IMAGINE THAT ONE VOTE IS OF NO IMPORTANCE! Every single one matters and yours might be the one to turn the Poll at an election. Generations of Irishwomen have longed to possess the weapon which has now been put into your hands. Show that you value it properly, and do your part in publishing to the world our determination to be free. Ireland demands this service of you; to ignore that demand would be treason.

Every woman of 30 is entitled to a Parliamentary Vote provided:
1. For six months before April 15th she has herself occupied either as owner or tenant a dwelling-house or land or business premises in the constituency. (In the case of business premises or land, the value of same must be £5.) It is sufficient to occupy part of a dwelling house, if the rooms are rented or unfurnished, or:
2. That she is the wife of a man who fulfils these conditions.

If the woman or her husband resides on premises by reason of employment, she is entitled to a vote, if the employer does not reside on the premises.

> Cumann na nBan Executive: *The Present Duty of Irishwomen*,
> c.1918. National Library of Ireland

WOMEN AS CANDIDATES FOR ELECTION

Constance Markievicz and Winifred Carney were the sole women candidates in the 1918 election. Kathleen Clarke, imprisoned in Holloway Jail, hoped to be a candidate, but discovered she had been a victim of internal political intrigue.

When I came out of prison, I heard the reason why I had not been selected or elected. I had been nominated by the North City, Dublin Comhairle Ceanntar (constituency council) for that area. When my name had been sent to Sinn Féin HQ for ratification, Harry Boland and Dick Mulcahy called on John R. Reynolds, Chairman of the Comhairle. They asked him to have my name withdrawn in favour of Dick Mulcahy, as I had been ratified as a candidate for Limerick City and I was sure of election there. John R. Reynolds told them that he had no power to do so, but that if the matter stood as they said he would summon a meeting of the Comhairle, and place the matter before them. The meeting was called and the matter put before it, and the members said they did not wish to change. According to Reynolds, Harry Boland told the meeting that literature was already out for my election in Limerick, and that I was sure of being elected there. The meeting very reluctantly agreed to the change.

Harry Boland was one of the Honorary Secretaries of the Sinn Féin Executive and must have known the exact position at the time, which was that Micheál Colivet had been ratified by headquarters as the candidate for Limerick City, and his election literature was already out. I was very angry when I heard all this but was glad to know it was not the fault of the people. My sisters knew all about it, and were also very angry. Dick Mulcahy was not then the well-known figure he became afterwards.

> (ed. Helen Litton): *Revolutionary Woman: Kathleen Clarke*, p.164

Hanna Sheehy-Skeffington was another woman many had hoped would be chosen to stand for election, as the letter from Rosamund Jacob makes plain.

I hope I'll soon see your name in the list of candidates in the Independent. I suppose the three women in jail will be put up too, though I see no sign of it at present – I hope the Dublin women at least are stirring themselves to get women candidates selected – women in most other parts of the country are too scattered to be able to do much, but the Dublin women ought to be able to insist on enough to get a start made anyhow. It seems to me the important thing for Irish suffragists to be doing at present. I hope they won't try to run women as independent candidates ... That would be hopeless everywhere, I should think, and would give the impression that they didn't care about the national issue.

Rosamund Jacob to Hanna Sheehy-Skeffington,
Sheehy-Skeffington Papers MS 24,108. National Library of Ireland

Constance Markievicz, a candidate for the St Patrick's constituency in Dublin, was the only woman to be elected. She was in Holloway Jail, together with Kathleen Clarke and Maud Gonne MacBride and therefore unable to campaign, but she sent out a brief election message to the Irish Women's Franchise League.

I received so few letters, since the Election campaign began that I begin to think the Censor is holding them up. I don't even know if my Election address was let pass ... One cannot but laugh at the delightfully fair way that this Election is being managed, our opponents making full use of the opportunities that are being lavished on them to misrepresent us in the press, and we are gagged and cannot answer them ... We wonder how long they will keep us and what is at the back of it all? I never feel that it matters much what happens to us, and I have a sure conviction that things are going all right for Ireland; we are only pawns in the game. I see that you and yours have been doing splendid work for me – One reason I'ld love to win is that we could make St Patrick's a rallying ground for women and a splendid centre for constructive work by women. I am full of schemes and ideas. Remember me to all my friends in the Irish Women's Franchise League.

Irish Citizen, January 1919

Winifred Carney, a member of the Irish Citizen Army, had acted as James Connolly's secretary in the GPO during the Rising. She stood on a 'Workers's Republic' platform for the Victoria division of Belfast. It was an impossible seat to win, and she received little support, as her letters to Joe McGrath make plain. Ironically, he later displaced Constance Markievicz as Minister for Labour after the split over the Treaty.

It is difficult to imagine you an MP. I was disappointed losing the £150 in my case, which would with workers on the day of the poll have been recovered. I had neither personation agents, committee rooms, canvassers or vehicles, and as these are the chief features in an election, it was amazing to me to find that 395 people went to the ballot on their own initiative, without any persuasion. The organisation in Belfast could have been better – much better. We had Fr O'Flanagan for 2 meetings, and Sean T. O'Kelly for one – that was the only help we got.

I wonder in time to come shall we occupy the same bench or shall you have become a Conservative while I remain an extreme anarchist because you see I am determined that I too shall one day share the responsibility in directing the Government of the country.

> Winifred Carney to Joe McGrath, 10 and 24 January, 1919.
> Quoted in Helga Woggon: *Winnie Carney, A Silent Radical*.

ELECTIONEERING
Although women realised the significance of ensuring that at least one representative of their sex was elected, nationalists – including Cumann na mBan – were involved in campaigning for many other constituencies. Meg Connery, vice-chair of the Irish Women's Franchise League, wrote a heated letter to Hanna Sheehy-Skeffington, criticising the failure to give more time to the Markievicz campaign.

Please tell the committee I couldn't take charge of Madame Markievicz's election in my present state of health – I have done many reckless things – but this is a little too reckless, even for me. The very nerve of Sinn Féin sets my teeth on edge. The one woman that they have thrown as a sop to the women of the country has her interest neglected and what is one to say of Cumann na mBan – surely it is their special duty to concentrate on the election of their own President! Why should the work be left to the chance care of 'outsiders' as they are so fond of calling us. They are too busy running after the the men the sea camp followers.

> Meg Connery to Hanna Sheehy-Skeffington,
> *Sheehy-Skeffington Papers* MS 22,684. National Library of Ireland

Hanna Sheehy-Skeffington had become a member of Sinn Féin as well as continuing her position as chair of the IWFL. However, she too was critical of the lack of effort being put into the Markievicz campaign.

Complaints have gone out not only from our members but from Cumann na mBan members and outsiders. Nonsense about books being given out. We applied at the first and day after day. Dozens of people called and one of the men was always away and he had all the books and another was drunk. Now I hear one has resigned and one dismissed ... I hear new management to take over from tomorrow ... It's the worst managed constituency in Dublin – every other constituency has had more frequent meetings (many nightly) and has been better canvassed. The committee can't play 'dog in the manger' so, finding them hopeless in cooperation, we decided, as I told you a week ago, to have our own meetings in future ... There are four meeting places, we have taken two. Committee can take them and take ours by having a different hour. As a woman's organisation we feel we have a duty in this matter and think it is a disgrace to the women's organisation if Madame Markievicz is let down by an inefficient committee...

Hanna Sheehy-Skeffington to Nancy Wyse-Power, 1919,
Sheehy-Skeffington Papers MS 24,091. National Library of Ireland

REACTIONS TO THE 1918 ELECTION:
The Irish Parliamentary Party, which had played a large part in defeating female suffrage measures in the House of Commons, was annihilated in the Sinn Féin landslide. This gave particular satisfaction to feminists. They were less pleased with women's underrepresentation.

There has been a great reshuffling of the political candidates. The old party of reaction has disappeared, and there was an element of ironic justice in the fact that women, whose claims it so long opposed with such unbending hostility, should have played so large a part in its final annihilation. Under the new dispensation the majority sex in Ireland has secured one representative. This is the measure of our boasted sex equality. The lesson the election teaches is that reaction has not died out with the Irish Party – and the Irish Women's Franchise League, which had been so faithful to feminist ideals, must continue to fight and expose reaction in the future as in the past. The events of the past year have strengthened our position – even a partial vote is a valuable weapon – and we must continue to consolidate our position, and keep the flag of sex equally flying. Great world changes are impending, systems of Government and systems of thought are dáily being cast into the melting pot. We see wider horizons opening everywhere before women. We must not be content with sops; we must march with the times. Whoever else has lagged or faltered, the place of the IWFL has always been in the van of liberty and progress.

Irish Women's Franchise League, Annual Report 1918:
Irish Citizen, April 1919

Some were determined to organise in order to ensure that women would be more adequately represented in future elections.

It was argued that women had neglected their opportunity at the late elections, and if a list of suitable women candidates had been prepared and furnished to all Ceanntar before the selection of candidates had commenced the women of Ireland would have more equitable representation in Dáil Eireann.

The Secretary was instructed to write to the Executive of Sinn Féin, furnishing a list of suitable members and urging that women be put forward for the double seats when they become vacant. The following were selected and the secretary instructed to ask their consent:

Mrs Sheehy-Skeffington, Dr Lynn, Mrs Clarke, Mrs Ceannt, Countess Markievicz, Miss Daly, Miss Carney, Miss Jacob, Miss Cashel.

Miss Plunkett for Pembroke Council, Miss Perolz for the Corporation and Dr Lynn for Rathmines Urban District Council were also discussed. Agreed to ask Mrs Sheehy-Skeffington if she would undertake a speaker's class. To write a circular to all county members urging on them immediate action in asking for names of suitable women candidates for positions vacant in their neighbourhood.

Minutes of Cumann na D'Teachtaire, 30 January 1919:
Sheehy-Skeffington Papers MS 21,194. National Library of Ireland

CUMANN NA mBAN CONVENTION 1918
The priority of Cumann na mBan remained military rather than political. At the Convention of 1918 provision was made to improve relationships with the Volunteers, and it was pointed out that the women were not 'Women's Sinn Féin Clubs', despite the fact that they worked to ensure Sinn Féin candidates were elected.

At the time of the Convention held in December 1917, the number of affiliated Branches was 100; it is now considerably over 600. This growth was due to the rapid spread of republicanism throughout Ireland; to the organising tours undertaken by the official Organiser, and by members of the Executive and others throughout the Provinces; and to the national uprising occasioned by the Conscription threat last springe ...

As a result of all this activity, Cumann na mBan not only possesses a larger number of Branches than ever before, but also these Branches are better organised and equipped and all have a clear idea of what membership of the organisation entails.

In February the Executive issued to Branches a circular entitled Military Activities, giving directions that for purposes of military organisation and in military operations, Captains of Branches should put themselves under the orders of the local Branch, and see that they are carried out. Also that the Captains of the Branches comprising a District Council should form a military Committee in touch with the Battalion Council in the event of military operations being necessary.

This step appeared to us desirable as it seemed at that time that the main reason for which we were established was in danger of being lost sight of. The spread of Sinn Féin Clubs and the series of by-elections, in which members of Cumann na mBan take a prominent part, occasioned an impression that our Branches were Women's Sinn Féin Clubs. Some confusion may still exist on this point in parts of the country, but things are much clearer than they were at the beginning of the year. The issue of this circular proved most opportune, as the British Government brought forward its Conscription proposals a few weeks later. The combined effect of the two events was to bring each Branch into complete co-operation with its local Volunteer Company. The Executive next issued directions for the making of First Field Dressings, and in most parts of the country the Volunteers are now supplied with them, also directions as to First Aid equipment for the members, storing of food, etce ...

Considerable financial assistance was also given to the Volunteers at this time: and we might mention that the members of the Dublin Branches, at the request of the Executive, in less than three weeks collected £296 for the arming and equipping of the Dublin Brigade.

When the English Parliament passed the 'Representation of the People' Act, the Executive felt that some steps should be taken towards seeing that the women of the country should not neglect securing the franchise to which they were now for the first time entitled. Accordingly a digest of the Act was made at Headquarters with the assistance of a legal friend, and a circular was issued to all Branches setting forth in the clearest possible terms the qualifications necessary for women voters, and directing local secretaries as to what steps they should take to secure the franchise for the women of their locality. Leaflets were also issued to Branches for distribution among women who were not members, setting out the reasons why their adherence should be given at elections to the Sinn Féin Partye ...

On July 4th a Proclamation was issued by Lord French, the Military Governor of Ireland, declaring Cumann na mBan, with other societies, to be an Association which 'encourages and aids persons to commit crimes, and promotes and incites to acts of violence and intimidation and interferes with the administration of the law and disturbs the maintenance of law and order.' The Proclamation declared further that the Association was a dangerous one. Orders were sent out immediately by the Executive that all Branches should carry on their usual work. No action has been taken to put the Proclamation into force, but two members of the Drumcondra Branch have served sentences of a month's imprisonment for distributing leaflets.

Addition to Preamble to Constitution:
Cumann na mBan is an organisation of women founded to advance the cause of Irish liberty. Although working in cooperation with other associations having the same objects, it is independent of them. Women of Irish birth or descent alone are eligible for membership.

Policy for 1918-1989
1. To follow the policy of the Republican Proclamation by seeing that women take up their proper position in the life of the Nation.
2. To develop the suggested military activities in conjunction with the Irish Volunteers.
3. To continue collecting for the 'Defence of Ireland' Fund, or for any other fund to be devoted to the arming and equipping of the men and women of Ireland.
4. To organise opposition to Conscription along the lines laid down in the two anti-Conscription Pledges:
   Denying the right of the British Government to enforce compulsory service in this country, we pledge solemnly to one another to resist Conscription by the most effective means at our disposal.
   (Women's Pledge):
   Because the enforcement of Conscription on any people without their consent is tyranny, we are resolved to resist the conscription of Irishmen.
   We will not fill the places of men deprived of their work through enforced military service.
   We will do all in our power to help the families of men who suffer through refusing enforced military service.

5. To assist in the movement to secure representation for Ireland at the Peace Conference, by the election of Republican Candidates, etc.

Cumann na mBan: *Convention Report, 1918*
National Library of Ireland

AN INTERVIEW WITH PRESIDENT WILSON

Mentioned in the Report of Cumann na mBan for 1918 was the fact that the 'most important piece of propaganda' done during the year was the presentation of the Cumann na mBan Memorial on Irish Freedom to President Wilson. This memorial had been forwarded to America before the last Convention met, but it was only in 1918 that it was handed to President Wilson by Hanna Sheehy-Skeffington, to whom, said the Report, 'we owe a great deal, as her persistence and courage wore down the efforts of English diplomacy to prevent her reaching the President. It is of interest to know that at the same time she presented President Wilson with a copy of the Republican Proclamation of Easter, 1916.' Hanna Sheehy-Skeffington gave her version of this meeting with the American President in a pamphlet published on her return to Ireland.

Sometime in January 1918, I received a mysterious paper (smuggled over, I cannot tell how, but certainly not 'passed by the Censor') from Cumann na mBan in Ireland, with a message that I was to deliver the paper personally into the President's own hands. It was a petition signed by Constance de Markievicz, President, Cumann na mBan, by Mrs Pearse, Mrs Wyse-Power, and many other distinguished Irishwomen. It put forth the claim of Ireland for self-determination, and appealed to President Wilson to include Ireland among the small nations for whose freedom America was fighting...

At first, the message that this petition was to be delivered personally rather dismayed me. In January, 1918, President Wilson was overwhelmed with work, and he had always been, even normally, one of the least accessible of Presidents. Still it was 'up to me' to formulate the request for a brief interview, and to work hard to get it. It was through the intermediary of Mr Bainbridge Colby, President of the Shipping Department, and of Mr Tumulty, the President's Private Secretary, that that request was granted. Three days after President Wilson formulated his now famous 'Fourteen Points' and on the day after the passing through Congress of the Federal Amendment for Women Suffrage throughout the States, I was accorded my interview – I was the first Irish exile and the first Sinn Féiner to enter the White

87

House and the first to wear there the badge of the Irish Republic, which I took care to pin in my coat before I went. The President had been busy all the morning receiving American suffragists who came from all over the country to thank him in person for his advocacy of their cause, and as it is generally admitted that the women of the West, enjoying a franchise, had cast an almost unanimous vote for Mr Wilson's election, it was appropriate that they should congratulate him on their further step towards the general enfranchisement of women.

The White House tradition is one of simplicity and democracy. Theoretically at least the first citizen of the Republic is at the service of the poorest and humblest citizen, and though in practice, and from the very nature of things, Presidents nowadays cannot emulate the simplicity of George Washington or Abraham Lincoln, still, enough of the tradition remains to permeate the White House atmosphere. Mr Asquith's butler, and possibly even Sir Edward Carson's, shows more 'side' and self-importance than President Wilson, who removes all embarrassment by a cordial handshake and a pleasant smilee ... Our interview was private – in fact, there is in the United States an un-written law precluding any report of an interview with the President, save that sent out by himself. The fact, however, of his 'friendly gesture to Ireland' in granting an interview to a declared Sinn Féiner was widely commented on by the friendly and the hostile press of the United States of America, also that he received a document unsubmitted to the British Censor, and that he consented to discuss and consider Ireland, was significante ...

After seeing the President I spent several months in Washington interviewing Senators and Congressmen on the Irish question, and everywhere I was met with friendliness and sympathy, the atmos-phere of Congress being more democratic and kindlier than the Tory clubroom of the British House of Commons. Most of all, it is an atmosphere more human and more courteous where women are concerned ...

On June 27th, 1918, I left for home, only to be held up at Liverpool. That story and the story of my subsequent internment in Holloway, I may not dwell upon just now, the exuberance of Lord French and Mr Shortt having nothing to do with the present narrative. My American mission was accomplished, and I could return home satisfied that I had tried to put the truth before the American people, and that I might trust to the international situation to do the rest.

Hanna Sheehy-Skeffington: *Impressions of Sinn Féin in America*,
pp. 27-30, Dublin, n.d.

AN APPEAL FOR PRISONERS

Although Irish women were not in agreement on all issues, the general opposition to British rule in Ireland led to important initiatives where women's united voice was very powerful. Suppression of organisations and censorship of the nationalist press meant that it was important for women to reach as wide an audience as they could.

Irishwomen's Appeal for Irish Prisoners

THIS statement, signed by representatives of various women's organisations in Ireland, has been sent to women's organisations on the Continent and America.

'We address this appeal to our sisters in other countries, asking them to use their influence to demand the formation of an International Committee of Inquiry, composed of men and women, who in the interests of humanity would send Delegates to inspect the prisons used for the detention of Irish political prisoners.'

Signed:

Cumann na mBan: Constance de Markievicz
Irishwomen's Franchise League: Hanna Sheehy-Skeffington
Irish Women Workers Union: Helena Moloney
Irishwomen's International League: Louie Bennett
Inghinidhe na h-Éireann: Maud Gonne MacBride
League of Women Delegates: Kathleen Lynn FRCSI

Irish Bulletin, 1 January 1920

CHAPTER 6

The War of Independence

THE HARDSHIPS OF WAR

A number of fact-finding commissions visited Ireland during the years of the war of independence. The Irish Women's Franchise League's address to delegates from America is typical of many hastily organised appeals for support.

To the Irish America Delegates

We, the members of the Irish Women's Franchise League, tender you a cordial welcome and wish your mission to secure self-determination for Ireland the happiest auspices. We as Irishwomen have suffered probably more than any other part of the community from the hardships imposed by alien militarism and we pray that we may be forever delivered therefrom. We recognise in you citizens of a republic many of whose states have granted citizenship to women. We too are proud of the fact that the Irish Republic in its Proclamation of Easter 1916, granted equal citizenship to men and women.

Signed by the Committee of the Irish Women's Franchise League.

Hanna Sheehy-Skeffington
Kathleen Keevey
Madame M. Gonne MacBride

Sheehy-Skeffington Papers MS 22,689. National Library of Ireland

THE AMERICAN COMMISSION ON CONDITIONS IN IRELAND

An American Commission on Conditions in Ireland heard evidence from witnesses in 1920-1. Their report was compiled by a Committee of One Hundred, which included Jane Addams, President of the Women's International League for Peace and Freedom.

Miss Ellen Wilkinson, Representative of the British Branch, Women's International League, 21 December 1920:

Q. 'Did you say that there is no sex crime in Ireland?'

A. 'Well, when we were there, we made very careful investigation, and we found no cases whatever of outrages on women ... We have had cases where women have been roughly handled, of course. And even that would happen where the men were sober; although such cases usually happened when the men were drunk. When I speak of rough treatment, I mean that the men come on in the middle of the night, and the women are driven from their beds without any clothing other than a coat; they are run out in the middle of the night and the house is burned. For women in delicate health that, of course, is terrible. And for women expecting children the mere fact of men coming like that and the nervous tension is terrible, of course.'

Sworn statement of Miss Ellie Lane of Ballingcollig, Co. Cork, 12 November 1920

A maid employed by Mr B.J. Magner, Ballincollig, she was in bed in one of the top rooms on the night of 29th September when the house was raided by armed, masked men. A big fellow came into her room after the others had searched:

'He made me sit down on the bed. I asked him what did he want me to do. Was it to assault me? He said no, but that I should get back to bed before he would leave. I refused. He then exposed his naked person to me and tried to seduce me by telling me he had plenty of money. I told him that I didn't want his money. He then told me to come into the Head Office in Cork and ask for Seamus – I told him I would not, but that I would clear out of Ballincollig the first moment I saw the daylight. The small chap was in the other girl's room all this time and watching into my room. The other girl was in bed, but no harm was done her. He called on the big chap to come away. They then left, and about half an hour afterwards Mrs Magner came and told us they were gone.'

Thomas Nolan, 14 January 1921

Several witnesses gave evidence that women suspected of being active Republicans had their hair cut off by the British forces.

'On the Sunday following (the case of Joe Cummins) they called at this house and called at Miss Madden and they cut off her hair. They also called at Miss Broderick's house and cut off her hair also; and they went to a house in College Road, the Misses Turk, and took the two of them out and cut off their hair. They also visited Miss

Burke's house. She was staying in Galway, working in a dry goods store, a house called McDonald's. She lived about 3 miles from the city of Galway. They went out there in the morning about half past five or six o'clock. A military lorry came, and she got out of bed and went out, and they went away. She thought when they went away that they might not come back again, and she went to bed again. She was not there a half an hour when they came back and cut her hair off. She was the sister of Father Burke.'

Q. 'Was there any reason given, for cutting off her hair?'

A. 'No reason whatever except that they were strong Republicans, all those girls.'

Q. 'Were they members of Cumann na mBan?'

A. 'Yes sir, they were members.'

Frank Dempsey, Mayor of Mallow, 19 January 1921

The IRA raided Mallow Barracks for arms and a sergeant major was killed during the attack, on 27 September 1920. In reprisal, the town hall, and a condensed milk factory, owned by the Cleeves family and employing five to six hundred people, were burned, also some houses in the town. About £300,000 of damages were done.

'Well, one woman, Mrs Connolly, who had a baby, about three days previous to this – she had to get up out of bed with her baby, of course. She got up, with nervousness and shock, and took her baby and remained out in the graveyard with her baby all night, with the result that she got pneumonia and died two or three days after this. The baby is alive yet. The next day most of the women in town were in hysterics and crying, all the next day. The state of the children was something fearful from this night of terror.

A local Relief Committee was formed to distribute money to those left jobless as a result of these actions. I can tell the Commission that when we started to distribute what we could every Saturday, practically all these houses – at least ninety five per cent of the houses that we went into in my portion of the town, they were nice, bright little homes; it would have done you good to go into them. Everyone seemed to take a pride in keeping their places as bright and nice as they could. Well, in six or eight weeks I have seen those homes destitute, and denuded of every bit of their furniture in order that they can give their children something to eat.'

American Commission on Conditions in Ireland, Interim Report:
Memorandum on British Atrocities in Ireland 1916-1920

'A CURFEW NIGHT IN LIMERICK'

Michael O'Callaghan, a former mayor of Limerick, was shot dead on 6 March 1921. In common with many other prominent figures in Sinn Féin he had received several death threats. His widow Kate, later elected to the Second Dáil, gave a graphic description of the night of her husband's murder.

On Tuesday, February 22nd, came a third raid later at night. Three women searchers came in, and in the glare I saw the garden full of troops, in full campaigning outfit. The women searched the wardrobes, drawers, and beds very carefully. Even the heels of my boots and shoes and the hems of my gowns were examined by the senior searcher, whose manner was insolent in the extreme.

On the night of Sunday, March 6th, Michael and I went to bed about 11 o'clock, after a very happy day ... later on, some relatives came in, and when they left before Curfew, Michael and I sat and read, or chatted by the drawing-room fire ... As we were going to sleep, I said: 'This has been a happy day.'

'Very happy indeed, thank God,' Michael replied.

I fell asleep ... .and was suddenly wakened by a tremendous knocking at the hall door.

I got out of bed, and threw up the window to ask: 'Who's there?'

It was a dark night, and I could see nothing. But a voice from the steps – and one that I knew – retorted, 'Who lives *here*?'

'Michael O'Callaghan!'

'We want him,' came at once – from two voices this time.

The thought came to me like a stab that such words preceded murder in Ireland at that time. I grew faint with horror, yet I spoke calmly enough.

'You can't see him at this hour of the night.'

The voice I knew came up again: 'We want him, so we're coming in anyhowe ... And we want the key of the gate.'

Michael was just then getting out of bed and I said to him, 'It's the usual thing. What shall I do?'

'I wish they wouldn't worry us like this,' he remarked. 'Ask them if there's an officer in charge ...'

'Oh, yes,' came the answer, 'two officers.' As I slipped on my dressing-gown and shoes, I'm afraid I cried a little. Michael said to me: 'Don't bother about Brigid tonight. You're nervous, so I'll come down with you this time. It's only the usual raid. Don't be afraid, dear.'

'I'll bring my rosary-beads,' I murmured. Michael had lighted a candle, and put on his gown and shoes. As we went down, I heard Brigid's door opening, and she told me afterwards she was surprised to see the master going down with me, in spite of all our arrangements. And Brigid heard him reassure me again on the stairs.

Michael lit the hall gas, and put the candlestick on the hall table. I warned him as I unlocked and unchained the door, and pulled it wide open.

When I saw two men with goggles and hats pulled down and coat collars high up about their ears, my heart leaped within me, *for I knew it meant murder!*

Both men cried out together, waving their revolvers at Michael, 'You come out here! ... Come out!'

My mind worked like a flame. I thought of the dark garden, of the river, and of all the nameless horrors... And stretching out both my arms to cover my husband, I pushed him back behind me, shouting: 'No, no – my God – not that!'

I heard Michael repeat: 'No, no,' just twice, and the men advanced after us menacingly along the hall. I caught at their hands as they tried to push me out of the way. There was a brief, confused struggle, and then the man on my right – he with the clear glasses and the blue eyes – suddenly freed his right arm and fired a shot over my shoulder.

I turned to see Michael stagger from the hall table and fall on to the mat at the foot of the stairs. In my agony I relaxed my hold of the man, and that same devil instantly slipped by me to empty his revolver into my dear husband's body as he lay on the floor. Meanwhile, I was struggling with the second man – he whose voice had brought me downstairs. But as the other, who had shot Michael, passed us to go out, I flew at him with the strength of a maniac. We three fought together in that hall, while I screamed with incoherent anguish. I battled with them both, as our feet slipped on the polished floor. My shoes fell off. I tore at the faces and heads of those assassins.

They never uttered a word, but beat me heavily on the head, shoulders and arms. We fell against the umbrella-stand. At last, with a savage effort, they threw me off, and I fell on my hip on the floor, screaming and helpless, while I watched the two men running over the garden grass in the shaft of light that streamed from the hall door ...

I crawled back to my husband, and fell across his body, with all my being crying out to my God to spare him to me. I had never before seen anybody die, so I continued to hope; whereas from the first shot there was no hope at all. Michael's eyes were closed, and he gave just one little sigh.

Mrs K O'Callaghan, 'A Curfew Night in Limerick',
in (ed.) W G Fitzgerald: *The Voice of Ireland*, pp. 147-50

THE WHITE CROSS

In December 1920 an American Committee for Relief in Ireland was formed to raise money to be sent to Ireland. In response the Irish formed the White Cross to distribute these funds to the estimated 100,000 people who had been left destitute. Maire Comerford, who had been working as secretary to the nationalist historian, Alice Stopford Green, became one of the people appointed to discover who was in need of assistance.

I did not experience the fury of the English terror campaign. I merely followed some of its tracks – within days or even weeks, and in daylight. I was not involved in the sense of having anything to lose, except, perhaps my own life or liberty. It was not my woman's lot to have those nearest to me killed, imprisoned with or without trial, 'on their keeping', or marching with the trench coated, disciplined, guerilla units of the IRA. No home was burned over my head. No children in my care depended on income or wages which a soldier of Ireland, or a prisoner had ceased to earn, or which a worker lost with the destruction of creamery or factory. I was not one of the 10,000 victims of the Belfast pogroms. This left me available when the Irish White Cross was founded. I was nominated – by whom I do not know – to be a member of its General Council.

Mother's diary shows that I went off for a tour for the White Cross on March 2nd 1921. I had a new Wexford-made Pierce bicycle all in order to eat up the roads in Connacht. I carried a letter for Mrs Geraldine Dillon, sister to Joseph Plunkett, wife of Professor Tommy Dillon UCG. I must have been tracked from Galway railway station because I was hardly inside the Dillon's house when the raiders came too.

Gerry had glanced at her letter, then, when the knock came to the door she thrust it down her neck. Unfortunately she was wearing a lacy kind of blouse and the paper showed through it and was seen. She was arrested on the spot. The result was that she was taken to Galway Jail. Dr Ada English TD and Alice Cashel were there too. I blamed myself for Gerry's arrest because I should have had the wit to know that anyone arriving in Galway off the Dublin train was liable to be followed.

The raiders had paid no attention to me but I was warned that they would certainly be back for me, and that I should make myself scarce. That evening I was guided across the railway lines and helped into a train from the wrong side. I had business in Loughrea with the Bishop of Cloyne, Dr Robert Browne, and also with Seamus Murphy, IRA. I spent the night, like many a better man or woman, in the workhouse, where Seamus's mother was matron. She was a very fine woman always ready to help wandering republicans on their way.

I called at the Bishop's Palace next morning – the greatest wet day in my memory; the water from my coat made embarrassing pools all around me on his polished floor. But the Bishop was friendly and he blessed my efforts in his diocese. He advised me that I should see His Grace of Tuam, the Archbishop. In Tuam Dr Gilmartin questioned me very closely about my work; he also gave it his approval.

These visits were necessary because personal relief had to be distributed through parish committees acting for the White Cross. My instructions insisted that the clergy must always supervise the collection of funds for the Society, and the awarding of relief to those qualified to receive it. It was my job to organise committees everywhere. All the religions existing in Ireland were represented on the governing body of the White Cross. The calls that I remember making were on Roman Catholic archbishops, bishops and clergy. They all consented to my operations, and some were cordial...

Every parish priest was a personality in his own right, and at that level my progress was very uneven. Some of the elder clergy had been supporters of the Parliamentary Party – probably in their youth fiery curates who had denounced Parnell. There were men among them who were as much opposed to the Republican cause as anyone could be who at the same time believed that Ireland should have Home Rule ...

Experience taught me to learn all the local facts, and to have my list of those who needed to be helped, before I approached the Parish Priest, except in cases where the people themselves had reliance on him in this particular connection.

Destitution was a new and terrible condition to be experienced by proud women; those who were in worst case were often least likely to advertise their predicament in unfriendly quarters. The bravest people can be too thin skinned to face a parish committee or submit to questioning about their means. I cannot forget my calls at the homes of fighting men, or dead men, where the wives, or widows were learning lessons which, too often, are behind the scenes of glory.

It was in their blood and tradition to suffer in the causes of national, religious and personal freedom. In many a home where children stood around silently, the issues at stake were clear enough. Mothers would face anything if only we could together win our present battle. The thought that they were rearing the first generation of children who would live their lives out in a free country was enough to support us. There the issue lay.

Máire Comerford: *Autobiography*.

LIFE IN DUBLIN

Maud Gonne lived in the centre of Dublin in the years 1918-22, an active publicist for the Irish cause. Her son Sean MacBride (here referred to as 'Seagan') was, unknown to his mother, involved with the IRA as well as studying law. Her daughter Iseult was about to give birth, and much of what she recounts in this letter to John Quinn, an old American friend, was similar to the experiences of many ordinary people trying to survive in Dublin at this time.

73 St Stephen's Green
21 February 1921

My dear friend

It is so long since I have seen or heard from you. What are you thinking? What are you doing? Here we are having a very strenuous and trying time, but the heroism and courage of every one makes one proud of being Irish. The English may batter us to pieces but they will never succeed in breaking our spirit. The spirit of the people in the devastated area is perhaps the most resolute of all. They are suffering untold horrors. I have seen and heard things far worse than in the war zones of France and Belgium. MrsDespard, Lord French's sister, has been staying with me.

She is a most remarkable woman and intensely Irish in feeling. We travelled together through the south of Ireland and with her I was able to visit places I should never have been able to get to alone, in the martial law areas. It was amusing to see the puzzled expressions on the faces of the officers and of the Black and Tans, who continually held up our car when Mrs Despard said she was the Viceroy's sister.

I enclose an article I have written which I would very much like if you could get into an American paper for me. I would like to get regular work [on] an American paper for articles on Ireland, as with the French change I am almost ruined. Could you introduce me to any editor or press agent?

We are very busy with work organising the Irish White Cross. The American Relief delegates are here now, do you know Mr France or Mr McCoy? The others are all Quakers. They are all very cautious timid people but I hope they will do good. Iseult (Mrs Stuart) is staying with me. Her baby will be born next month. Luckily her nerves are pretty good, for Dublin is a terrible place just now. Hardly a night passes that one is not woke up by the sound of firing. Often there are people killed, but often it is only the crown forces firing to keep up their courage. One night last week there was such a terrible fusilade just outside our house, that we all got up thinking something terrible was happening. That morning, when curfew regulations permitted us to go out, we only found the bodies of a cat and dog riddled with bullets.

Seagan is working at his law course in the National University. There again it is hard for boys to work, with raids and arrests among the students going on continually. The English are particularly down on the students. Lots of them are in jail. One quiet boy of 17, a divinity student, Lawlor, was beaten to death by the Black and Tans.

Do write me a long letter. Tell me what you think of it all, and if America is likely to protest against all these horrors.

Seagan and Iseult join me in sending you kindest regards.

Always your old friend,

Maud Gonne MacBride

Berg Collection, New York Public Library

ARREST – TWO EXPERIENCES
With large numbers of undisciplined Black and Tans mobilised to counteract the republican forces, the dangers involved in arrest were terrifying. Linda Kearns, a nurse who was a Cumann na mBan activist during the War of Independence and the Civil War, described her experience. She was later sentenced to ten years imprisonment, the longest sentence passed upon a woman.

Every detail of my arrest is vividly implanted in my memory – never to fade from it. The brain sometimes receives certain impressions so deeply that they are, as it were, seared into our very mind, and so remain, never to grow fainter, or to become dimmed as the years pass.

Carrying, as I had done now for some years, my liberty – and I might say my life, too – in my hands dáily and hourly, and having escaped capture for so long, I had become more or less case-hardened, and if not reckless, at least somewhat impervious to danger. And so I had grown to regard my arrest as a rather unlikely contingent, indeed I had begun to hardly think about it at all. And yet in the end it came very swiftly and suddenly. I was driving my car on the night of November 20th, 1920, at about 11.30 p.m. The car contained, besides myself, three young men and a certain amount of 'stuff' – 10 rifles, 4 revolvers, and 500 rounds of ammunition, to be exact. It was a very dark night, and we were going steadily along the quiet country road. My hands were on the wheel, my eyes looking ahead, intent only on my driving, when suddenly, like a thunder-clap, came the order to halt. How clearly it all comes back to me – the surrounding darkness, which our lights made more black, the men sitting tensely beside me, and the the silence broken by the sharp, quick word – 'Halt!' And again – 'Halt! Damn you, halt!'

I stopped the car, and we were immediately surrounded by a crowd of the most savage and undisciplined men which it has ever been my misfortune to meet. They were all drunk, shouting and talking together, and no one seemed to be in command. They were a mixed lot, comprising military, police, and Black and Tans. My three companions were at once pulled violently out of the car and searched, and the automatic pistol which the Commandant had in his possession was taken from him immediately. The three of them were very badly used, and it was impossible not to admire them for their coolness and self-control.

All was confusion and darkness, save where the lights of the cars revealed now and again some of their drunken and savage faces. Various orders were given and countermanded. Some one shouted: 'Shoot them!' and shots were fired around us. I heard one of my companions say: 'Don't shoot the girl!' but one of the police said: 'Oh, we can't leave her to tell the tale!' The boys with me gave their names and addresses, one of them adding that he was a soldier of the Republic, for which he got a blow across the face, and in spite of my own hazardous position I was constrained to admire him, he behaved with such courage and coolness. Indeed, all three of my comrades were splendid, and all their thoughts even then were for me.

Meanwhile, the noise made by the Crown forces was deafening – it was like Bedlam let loose, and there was no discipline amongst them, for the Head Constable in charge of the police and Black and Tans seemed to have absolutely no control over his men, while the officer in charge of the khaki-clad lot appeared afraid to give them an order. This pandemonium went on for about half an hour, and then I was put into my car and driven away in the company of three men, either police or Black and Tans, I do not know which, as the confusion and noise were very stupifying. The others were flung into the lorry, and we all met later in the barracks, No. 2, in Sligo.

I shall never forget the scene in the day-room of that barrack! The prisoners were just thrown in by force ... My own leather overcoat, gloves, wristlet watch, and signet ring were taken forcibly from me, and never returned. In the centre of the room was a table, on which was a strange mixture of rifles and ammunition, whiskey and porter! The men came in and out continually, and would knock off the head of a bottle of stout, and drink it without a glass, and they drank the whiskey neat from the bottle. As a result, they were all more or less intoxicated, some of them so bad that they were more like fiends than human beings. After a while the Head Constable's daughter came and searched me, and I was then taken to a 'lock up' – a tiny room, with a hard bench and stone floor, and it was most bitterly cold on that November night.

But even here I was not left long in peace. The tormentors brought one of my late companions past my door and then fired several shots, to make me think that he was killed. Then they consulted outside my door in loud voices as to whether they would 'shoot the girl next, or do for one of the other fellows first.' This went on for some time for my benefit, to terrify me, as I knew. But it was trying on the nerves, especially as I knew well that they could shoot me with impunity if they took the notion to do so at any time. Then I was questioned, threatened, and finally offered bribes. They came in groups of three or four to question me, and to see if they could identify me; and during all this time they called me all sorts of names – I was a 'murderer,' and a 'driver of murderers!' One often hears and reads of nights of horror; well, I can say truthfully that I have passed through one. At 7 a.m. next morning I was brought to the day-room and again questioned. I asked for my overcoat and rug, but they refused to return them to me.

We were then brought to Sligo Jail.

Annie M P Smithson (ed.): *In Times of Peril: Leaves from the Diary of Nurse Linda Kearns from Easter Week, 1916 to Mountjoy*, pp. 15-18.

Eithne Coyle, President of Cumann na mBan from 1926, was arrested by the Black and Tans after many months of active service.

Our main work was to act as couriers and to carry arms, going all over the place on our bicycles. This we could easily do; the fashions were long at that time and police checks were not very frequent upon girls.

I was eventually arrested by the Tans at a place called Ballagh, in Co. Roscommon, where I had a little house to myself. They came first and they raided, and I said, thanks be to God, they're evidently not going to arrest me. I was not as careful as I should have been; I should have made off there and then, because they came again the next morning at 4 a.m. and this time they held me. I was brought into a barracks in Roscommon. I shall never forget how cold it was. It was the first of January, 1921, and their method of cleaning out the cell was to take buckets of freezing water in and swill them around the floor. It was then swept out with a yard-brush. Was I glad when eventually I was sent on to Mountjoy where I was charged before a field-general courtmartial. It was presided over by three military officers.

They sentenced me to one year's imprisonment for activities prejudicial to the Defence of the Realm. They had got no arms nor documents upon me; I took very good care of that, but they knew I had been working with the Volunteers. I had been in Roscommon ostensibly organising for the Gaelic League, and as all the Volunteers were interested in the language it was a good cover. I had been there for six months, seconded from Dublin. Our OC was Pat Madden. They were a good Republican family, and all of them remained anti-Treaty afterwards. There was a small unit of Cumann na mBan there, and of course I was in it, as was Pat's sister. He often came by my cottage, and would leave in a gun or two if he was going someplace where he felt he ought not bring them. I suppose I was under the microscope of the RIC, being a stranger and hooking around everywhere on my bicycle. I used carry despatches into Roscommon town or north to Athleague. I had plenty of narrow shaves. Travelling at night you had to have a lamp. In that way they could nab you easily as they might be on foot patrol. But if you heard the lorry you could stop and throw the bicycle over the ditch. They charged me with possession of innocent Cumann na mBan documents and with having a plan of a barracks. But that was not got on me; it was found in someone else's possession.

Uniseann MacEoin (ed.): *Survivors*, pp. 152-3

REPUBLICAN COURTS

Dáil Eireann, the Irish Parliament set up after the elections in 1919, established its own system of local government and arbitration courts which were intended to supplant the British system that still operated in Ireland. It often fell to women to ensure that republican courts had sufficient personnel to operate them. And guidelines laid down after women's intervention within Sinn Féin ensured that women justices were an important element in the system, as Constance Markievicz's brief account confirms.

The Republican Justices were to be elected in compliance with the old Gaelic custom.

I presided over the election in my constituency, and can vouch for facts. Representatives were called from the Republican Army, Cumann na mBan (the women's army), from all the Trades Unions, and Labour organisations, from the clergy, from the Jews, and from all available organisations and in addition from persons connected with other interests who could be trusted not to betray us to the Black-and-Tans, who would have been only too glad to have raided our meeting. These people, after careful consideration of each person suggested, elected the panels of justices. Those elected were chosen irrespective of sex or age, because those who knew them believed that each one would be just and that each one would have the courage to carry on the work – in spite of the perils attached to it.

> Constance Markievicz: 'What Irish Republicans Stand For',
> leaflet. Reprinted from *Forward*, Glasgow, 1923

Because of conditions under which the courts operated, few have left any record of their experiences. The evidence collected by Máire Comerford gives us an invaluable insight into those times.

I know what I know about the Republican courts – local and incomplete knowledge – from my friends who took part as justices, and police, and also in organising them. Mrs Aine Heron, of Belmont Avenue, Donnybrook, was a brave, splendid woman who had a big growing family. Work for the courts suited her because she could do it while the children were at school.

She was present at the first meeting to inaugurate a court for the Pembroke area of County Dublin. This was in Madame O'Rahilly's house, 40 Herbert Park, Ballsbridge on March 2nd, 1919. Pembroke anticipated the establishment of Mr De Valera's Ministry on April 2nd and the Dáil Decree establishing Arbitration Courts, 18th June, and the escape of the Minister for Home Affairs from prison in October. It provides one more piece of evidence that the country had taken the bit in its teeth at that time...

Mrs Hanna Sheehy-Skeffington described the working of the South City Courts at a more advanced stage ... The justices: 'administered a ready-made code of justice; they were elected through the Organisation (Sinn Féin), and the panel included a number of public spirited priests. They were formed into panels according to districts and were summoned to act in turn, it being the practice to have three together, one usually a woman, and one a clergyman...a network of panels was spread over the country to the western islands ... Uniformity was maintained through a central office on the quays, known to only a few, for of course the whole machinery was "illegal".'

I know from both of them that Mrs Eamon Ceannt and Mrs Heron sometimes sat together. On one occasion their decision was set aside by the Minister. Cases had been brought against a number of women by a money lender who was also the proprietor of a grocery shop. The defendants had borrowed his money to buy food in his shop. The Justices calculated that he was getting 800% on his investment. They dismissed the prosecutions against the women and they announced they would do the same thing on all similar occasions. It was their view, they announced, that thriftless people would not be stopped from borrowing at exorbitant rates until moneylenders were discouraged from lending. Austin Stack refused to countenance their decision. He told them they were there to enforce law and they had departed from it.

Mrs Heron spoke of the solicitors and barristers who were generally in court. On one occasion she pulled one of them up when he was cross-examining. 'We will have no brow beating here' she told him. 'May I not cross examine?' he asked. 'You may cross-examine, but you must be fair. This is not a British court', she told him.

Justices were sometimes allotted to Countess Markievicz, Minister for Labour, or others who were substituting while she was in prison. Mrs Eamon Ceannt told me of her first appearance as official Arbitrator in a Labour Court at Kilrush, Co. Clare. 'I was conducted to a high chair in the Rural District Chamber and I had my heart in my mouth.' Each side had solicitors. When she asked what was the procedure they bowed, and said 'Whatever Madam decides.' She had other cases, in Fermoy, Millstreet and Castleconnell.

Máire Comerford, *Autobiography*

THE *IRISH BULLETIN*

In 1919 the Dáil set up a Department of Publicity. All nationalist newspapers and many ordinary papers had been suppressed so it was decided to establish a news-sheet, aimed primarily at international opinion. Kathleen McKenna was appointed typist for the Irish Bulletin. *Other figures she refers to are: Robert Brennan (Bob), Frank Gallagher (Gally), Arthur Griffith (AG), Desmond Fitzgerald (Desmond), Anna Fitzsimons (Fitzie).*

My task would be to type, and make mimeographed copies of the proposed news-sheet, and be responsible, under all circumstances, for its distribution by hand to friendly persons in Dublin, and, through the post, to the sympathisers with our cause, at home and abroad, who would agree to receive it, and make use of its contents in their writings.

Mr Brennan warned me that anything could happen to me at the hands of the British should I be captured by them, but added that with my presence of mind, keen power of judgement and observation and *sang froid*, I would learn to dodge, bluff and baffle them.

My colleague was Anna Fitzsimons (later Mrs Frank Kelly) whose task was to get from the dáily press items of news suitable for publication, as well as for use in compiling the weekly summary of

British atrocities in Ireland which Kathleen always prepared. Michael Nunan, Fianna member, acted as office boy...

I put a stencil into my typewriter, typed the words 'The Irish Bulletin Vol. 1 No 1. 11 November 1919'. The three men stood near me: three pairs of critical eyes were fixed upon my fingers as they danced unerringly over the keyboard. Down in Harcourt Street the crowds were cheering and singing 'Soldiers are we whose lives are pledged to Ireland', and I was happy, for now I, too, was a soldier playing my humble part in my country's fight for freedom. THE FIRST COPY: I fixed the stencil to the duplicator and rolled off the first clear copy; the men were delighted with it, and with themselves. The *Irish Bulletin* had been born. Griffith said I was its god-mother. During the twenty terror-filled hunted months in which, on a point of honour, its publication never once failed, I guarded my god-child with jealous affection.

... That same evening Michael delivered envelopes containing copies of the first edition of the *Irish Bulletin* to the Dublin newspaper offices and to hotels where friendly correspondents of foreign newspapers were staying. I dropped others, in batches of two's and three's so as not to arouse suspicion, into various red pillar-boxes throughout the city. Next morning the Irish press carried extracts from it ...

'Fifth Hideout': Early in the New Year, 1920, Mrs Larry Nugent agreed to give the Propaganda Department of Dáil Eireann a flat on the upper floor of her home in Upper Mount Street. She kindly placed two large well-lighted rooms and some tables and chairs at our disposal. Here, Desmond, Bob, Gally, Fitzie, Michael and myself were happily reunited and, although the house was also the refuge, day and night, of some of the most active gunmen of the Dublin Brigade, we spent there the most pleasant period of our adventurous career. The little box duplicator was still functioning to perfection but with the increased number of pages – sometimes five or six – and the increased number of persons eager to receive the Bulletin and use its interesting and enlightening contents, it took many hours to complete each issue. When the evening rush of mail-time came, everybody, even the callers, gave a 'hand' at clipping papers together, folding and packing and a 'tongue' at 'licking' stamps and envelopes.

The callers were many and most interesting. Countess Markievicz, Minister for Labour, was one of the most frequent and most welcome. She would sit for hours on a corner of a table smoking cigarette after cigarette and discussing in her musical voice the most varied and fascinating topics. She was a very beautiful and charming lady, bubbling over with enthusiasm and confidence in Ireland's future ... Another visitor was Maud Gonne MacBride; she too, a tall, stately woman, clothed in black from head to foot, the woman whom Yeats had loved and who inspired many of his works.

With the reinforcement of the British military in March, 1920, by 12,000 'Black and Tans' and 1,000 Auxiliary police, a veritable reign of terror began. Day by day our secretly circulated paper made known such alarming information concerning the uncontrolled activities of these agents of the British Crown that the hunt to locate our den became ever more intense and ever more intense, too, grew our precautions to shield it, and our anxiety for its fate...

Towards the end of the summer the locality in which our 'hide out' was situated had become one in which notorious British spies were living and working. Nugent's was a house in which hunted volunteers, actively engaged in the guerilla warfare, found refuge. Armoured cars and Crossley tenders prowled around the zone during curfew, and we were warned that on a few occasions, suspicious looking individuals were observed loitering around Nugent's. One night Fitzie, who had considered it was unsafe to sleep in her Hume Street digs, spent the night in the front room of our department, only to be alarmed by the rays of search-lights focused pryingly on the windows. I was advised 'to hop' with the Bulletin, while 'the hopping' was good. And it was well I did so, for shortly after we evacuated Nugent's it was subjected to a terrifying raid.

...My duties were now no longer confined to preparing the Bulletin and ordinary secretarial work. They had become manifold, difficult and fraught with ever-increasing dangers. Owing to Molesworth Street being in the heart of the city we advised our friends, both for their own sakes and ours, to refrain from visiting us. AG no longer called, and one of my tasks was to meet him, when he was not in gaol, by appointment, either on the upper floor of the Bailey, or in the Sod-of-Turf tea rooms, situated not far distant from our hide-out. The Irish Book Shop, in Dawson Street, was a convenient place where I could drop in, take down a book and read whilst waiting to convey, or receive, messages and documents far from inquisitive eyes.

Usually during the late afternoon I cycled across the city, sometimes having to negotiate military hold-ups, to call at 'The Dump' ... to collect, or restitute, correspondence between our and other Dáil Departments as well as material useful for inclusion in the Bulletin ... I concealed the stuff I conveyed in a series of spacious pockets sewn into an underskirt...

The winter we spent in Molesworth Street was an exceptionally wet and cold one. Owing to the need for secrecy we could not request the caretaker, whom we did not yet trust, to clean the flat and light fires. Often the duplicating ink froze in the tubes and we had to resort to burning twisted-up pages of the bulky London *Times* to thaw out both it and our stiff fingers ... Fitzie and I resorted to the ruse of putting blotting paper beneath our stockings to dry them and keep us warmer. But we were always in good spirits; we were excellent colleagues who pulled together in perfect harmony; each knew his own work and did it, putting into it every atom of energy and faith. We skipped meals, when necessary; we stayed on working until the last safe minute prior to curfew; nothing was counted a hardship or sacrifice. At the post hour rush we all united in the despatch room; then cold, damp, hunger, fatigue were forgotten...

The sentiments of the members of our little Bulletin staff were rather mixed the day 'the truce broke!' On the whole, we did not appreciate it, for we realised that it meant the termination of a period, and of a staunch comradeship, that was unique, precious and dear.

Together with the last Special issue, Gally prepard an 'extraordinary issue!' It was not typed by me, but inscribed by Gally on a stencil!! It was headed 'MAKERS OF THE REPUBLIC'; beneath was a bellicose figure of myself – THE DAIL GIRL – wielding a cudgel in one hand and a revolver in the other. Further down the sheet was a very tall, thin figure carrying an attaché case – THE MERE PRESIDENT. The page was decorated with tricolours intertwined with union jacks, fireworks and the words 'Tigan Tu?' 'Yes Mate!'

We rolled off this last edition of the *Irish Bulletin* and kept copies of it in memory of the happiest days of our lives. The mission of the *Irish Bulletin* had been faithfully carried through. With a tear and a sigh I whispered 'Béannact De leat a leinbh' to my twenty month old god-child.

Kathleen McKenna: 'The *Irish Bulletin*'.
The Capuchin Annual 1970, pp. 503-27

CUMANN NA mBAN CONVENTION 1921

As Cumann na mBan was a proscribed organisation, the 1920 Convention was conducted in difficult circumstances and no details were reported. At the 1921 Convention, which took place during the period of the 'Truce', their President, Constance Markievicz, recently released from jail, paid tribute to her members' contribution.

President's Address

I say to each and every one how proud and glad I am to be among you again, and how pleased I was when I came out of prison in meeting my friends – many of them Volunteers – to hear all of the great work Cumann na mBan had done while I was in Mountjoy doing nothing at all. I want to tell you how proud I am of the girls who stood in the gap of danger during the time of stress and war last winter. There was a generous chorus of praise from all parts of Ireland for the girls of Cumann na mBan on the way they have worked through the winter. Their courage, their capacity, and above all their discretion, were praised to me. These girls did daring and brave things that nobody ever heard of from anyone. I think this is the biggest praise I can give you today. The capacity too and the training as well as discretion and also the courage of those who were under fire, all deserve great praise. When the history of Ireland is to be written the name of Cumann na mBan will be a name that will go down to your children and your children's children, and as an organisation will stand as a memorial to the Irish people as a great organisation of the past. That is what I have been told about you and that is what I want to tell you today.

I have very little more to say to you. This as we all realise is a time for action not talk, but we must think of the future. Don't think it is going to be peace. Go out and work as if the war was going to break out next week. That is my message to you. Our strength lies in the fact that we are ready to fight. What has been won has been won by the fighting men and women of Ireland and no one else. The men in the country tell me they never could have carried on without the help of Cumann na mBan who did all sorts of work for them. Action again I say is most important, as if the enemy sees any weakening the whole thing is up. When you go away from here, go and prepare yourselves to do good work for Ireland in the way you have done it in the past.

Put yourselves in touch with your local Volunteers, avoid quarrelling, look over deficiencies, and try and work everywhere together wherever you can ...

Secretary's Report

Since the last Cumann na mBan Convention, held under war conditions last October, our country has come through a tremendous ordeal and come through it triumphantly. There can be no hesitation in saying that our organisation played no small part in the struggle and it too has come through triumphantly. Last year at our Convention we had only about 120 delegates – today we have nearly 400. Last year our affiliated branches numbered 300 – today they number nearly 800 ...

There is no need for me to explain to you under what circumstances the work was carried on – most of you are only too familiar with the story – raids, arrests and imprisonments were not confined to any one part of Ireland. Several of our Executive members including the President, served sentences and one at least – Miss MacGrane is still in prison. Branch officers and the rank and file have suffered too – during the past year more than 50 women have been through prison and to all these we extend our congratulations on the stand they have made and our assurance that should the occasion arise again we are all ready to face what they have been through. Not alone to those who have been in prison do we extend congratulations – we do it to all those outside who did their duty quietly and determinedly and especially to those in the war areas who gave such magnificent help to the IRA.

'In my area,' writes the Commandant of the 1st W. Div. 'there was no question of the girls only helping. In despatch carrying, scouting, and intelligence work, all of which are highly dangerous, they did far more than the soldiers. In addition to this the Flying Columns would have collapsed early this year were it not for the assistance of the women, organised and unorganised. They fed the men, clothed them, supplied them with tobacco and everything else they needed. Where they got enough money to do all this was a mystery to me, but they did it. When almost everybody deserted us during the Xmas panic these girls stood by us and at the height of the terror we found that the more dangerous the work the more willing they were to do it.'

... But after so much glowing praise we must not be deluded into thinking we are perfect. There are a few points to which I must direct your attention and which argue a certain carelessness, and lack of proper discipline. The first deals with orders and despatches from H.Q. ....

... And finally, we would appeal to all our members to remember their work is for Ireland always, and that all trivial disputes and side issues should only get their proper value. We do not know yet whether we are to have peace or war. Let the truce time be well spent in strengthening our organisation – in improving our discipline and in making our position impregnable.

Propaganda Report

Our efforts at propaganda during the year took two definite directions – one, and our main one, was to keep up the morale of the civilian population and to let it be clearly understood that all Ireland was behind its army, no matter what the consequences. The other was to put our case before other countries. Miss McGrane was made D/Propaganda, but after her imprisonment in January, the work was carried on by Mrs Mulcahy and Mrs Fitzgerald with the collaboration of other members of the Executive.

Towards the first end – the home propaganda – most of our energies were devoted. Before Xmas the Irishwomen and the IRA leaflet was printed and distributed under great difficulties. A similar leaflet with a few suitable alterations was issued to all members of the British House of Commons and to a large number of foreign journalists.

In January large posters and smaller handbills of the Stand Fast leaflet were sent through the country. A number of places through the country notified us that they could if supplied with drafts of leaflets get printing done for their own area and this they did afterwards.

In February 50,000 Stand Fast leaflets were given letter box distribution in Dublin.

In March shortly before Easter a further leaflet in large posters and small handbills was circulated through the country. Owing to enemy activity this did not reach its destination in all cases.

Our second aim – to put our case before other countries – was carried out at the same time. In America, Miss McSwiney at our request spoke for us as representing the Republican Women of Ireland. We sent her copies of the leaflets we were distributing here, and we also sent them to women's organisations in America. Members of our Executive always interviewed foreign [journalists] – English or otherwise – who came here to learn the truth about Ireland, and put before them clearly the attitude of the women in the fight ...

The Dublin Branches did special Propaganda work for the IRA. In April and May the operations of the Dublin Brigade for these months were posted thickly all over the city and this at a time when the streets were infested with spies and with armed patrols ...

In conclusion, I would call the attention of the Delegates to the fact that Peace is not yet definitely secured. There is still work and plenty of work for the women of Ireland to do in propaganda as well as in other things. We must see to it that there is no lowering of the Flag – no celebrating before the Victory is assured ...

Cumann na mBan, *Convention Report 1921*,
National Library of Ireland

CHAPTER 7

Civil War

WOMEN AND THE DAIL DEBATE ON THE TREATY

The debate over the Treaty was lengthy and deeply emotional. Four of the six female members of the Second Dáil were women who had lost male relatives during the past years of war, but all rejected accusations that their opinions were warped because of their personal sorrows. The following are extracts from both the private and the public sessions of the Dáil debates.

Mrs Pearse

Mrs Pearse said she was probably the oldest member in the House. She had been elected here on account of her beloved boys. She was very happy she had been elected, though she was almost an ornament here, so that the name of a Pearse would be in the first Irish Parliament. But as her beloved boy had stated at the graveside of O'Donovan Rossa they were an unconquered and an unconquerable nation. She wanted to say the same and she trusted and hoped they would remain so. She felt grateful to their beloved President and to all those in charge of their destiny for the manner in which they had dealt with the negotiations and she felt confident they were safe in the Ministry's hands. She stood for the one thing, and she was sure she was voicing the sentiments of the other women members also, what their men in Easter Week died for, and that was an Irish Republic.

Private Session, 14 September 1921

Countess Markievicz

I am a Republican, I won't say a die-hard, I say an undying Republican, and to me, in that Treaty, you absolutely and deliberately by swearing an oath to the King of England, put the Republic behind you. You, as it were, pledge yourself to an authority other than the Irish Republic ... .I will swallow any humiliation but I will not do a thing which I would consider dishonest, first, before God and my own soul and, secondly, before the men who died for Ireland in all the generations and thirdly, to my constituency in St Patrick's and the poor and the humble. They are nearly all poor now and each one has said to me, 'You will be true to the Republic.'...I wish to say that I hope that the end of this long disagreement in which we have all taken part will be that we can all work together for the good of Ireland ... If we don't get now some compromise, some loyal pledge that we can stand all toget-her in the name of the dead and of Ireland, we shall break up all that has been done, ruin the cause for which so many have risked their lives, for which our men died and were tortured ... I ask you to be quite loyal and true to what you believe is right and if we do that I think we shall throw the enemy out of our country. I shall have more to say on the Treaty tomorrow, but this is not the time to say it.

Private Session, 16 December 1921

Mary MacSwiney
At the outset I should like to say that I must ask from the members of the Dáil for forgiveness if I speak too long. I stand here tonight in the name of the dead to ask the men of this Assembly, and I know I need not wish [sic] the women, every one of you to face your consciences tonight to ask yourselves if you are going to disunite this country, to create a split where we had been most perfectly united to all appearances, at all events, whether we are going on Monday, before the world, a watching, waiting, anxious world, to act together by a large majority so that there need be no questioning if or whether we are going to split this Assembly into two halves and drive the country back again for a generation, and as Deputy Liam Mellows has already pointed out there is only one way of doing that and that is the way of principle ... I have said that I stand here in the name of the dead ... I do not speak of my right any more than I do of others to allude to those who have gone but I ask those here tonight who are putting expediency before principle to kindly leave the names of the dead out of their speeches. I consider myself in a different position from most of those who have suffered, for every other person who lost one near and dear to her lost him suddenly, I did not. For 74 days I eat [sic] a thought and let me tell you in 74 days you have much time for thinking. I weighed the cost, I weighed every thought. I am not a fool though I have been told I was a fool if I thought this Dáil did not mean to compromise. I do not think I am a fool and sitting there by that death bed the like of which has never been known in the world before I looked at this question which we are facing tonight from every possible angle from the orthodox point of view, from the national point of view, and I asked myself, when talking with my dying brother I asked him, was it worth the cost, and we decided it was, and one of the last things he ever said to me was, 'Thank God

there will be no more compromise now ... Who, six years ago, could have expected this country could have produced at a moment's notice statesmen and soldiers of the highest quality, and that our Cabinet and those who have acted for us in this matter have been the wonder of the world? Our soldiers have commanded admiration of the world, and I am glad that the world has not been listening to some of them today. Who could have expected six years ago that men drawn from all kinds of life, clerks and professors, and plain teachers, and I don't know what business or profession half of them were. But who were they six years ago? Nobodies, and today they stand in a position commanding the admiration of the world, and they stand on it because they stood on the rock of principle and if they compromise they go down in the admiration of the world and they go down absolutely in the admiration of their own people, for say what you like about this Treaty, it is a compromise of principle. We have heard a great deal about war tonight and the horrors of war. You men that talk need not talk to us about war. It is the women who suffer, it is the women suffer the most of the hardships that war brings. You can go out in the excitement of the fight and it brings its own honour and its own glory. We have to sit at home and work in more humble ways, we have to endure the agony, the sunshines, the torture of misery and the privations which war brings, the horror of nightly visitations to our houses and their consequences. It is easier for you than it is for us, but you will not find in Ireland a woman who has suffered who today will talk as the soldiers here today have talked, and I ask the Minister for Defence, if that is the type of soldier he has, in heavens's name send the women as your officers next time.

Private Session, 17 December 1921

Mrs O'Callaghan
I rise to support the President's motion for the rejection of these Articles of Agreement, and, lest anybody should afterwards question my right to stand here and criticise and condemn this Treaty, I want it to be understood here and now that I have the clearest right in the world. I paid a big price for that Treaty and for my right to stand here. The last Deputy talked about indecent rattling of the bones of the dead in this assembly. Since I came up to Dublin for this Session I have been told, with a view to changing my vote, I suppose, that my husband was never a Republican. I challenge any Deputy in this Dáil to deny my husband's devotion to the Republic, a devotion he sealed with his blood. I would ask the gentlemen who say he was never a Republican, but who say they are Republicans, and intend to vote for this Treaty, to leave my husband's name out of the matter. I have been told, too, that I

have a duty to my constituents. They, I am told, would vote for this Treaty, and I ought to consider their wishes. Well, my political views have always been known in Limerick, and the people of Limerick who elected me Deputy of this Dáil two months after my husband's murder, and because of that murder, know that I will stand by my convictions and by my oath to the Irish Republic. There is a third point I want to clear up. When it was found that the women Deputies of An Dáil were not open to canvass, the matter was dismissed with the remark: 'Oh, naturally, these women are very bitter.' Well, now, I protest against that. No woman in this Dáil is going to give her vote merely because she is warped by a deep personal loss. The women of Ireland so far have not appeared much on the political stage. That does not mean that they have no deep conviction about Ireland's status and freedom. It was the mother of the Pearses who made them what they were. The sister of Terence MacSwiney influenced her brother, and is now carrying on his life's work. Deputy Mrs Clarke, the widow of Tom Clarke, was bred in the Fenian household of her uncle, John Daly of Limerick. The women of An Dáil are women of character, and they will vote for principle, not for expediency. For myself, since girlhood I have been a Separatist. I wanted, and I want, an independent Ireland, an Ireland independent of the British Empire, and I can assure you that my life in Limerick during 1920, culminating in the murder of my husband last March – my life and that event have not converted me to Dominion status within the British Empire. I would like to say here that it hurts me to have to vote against the Minister for Foreign Affairs. He was a friend of my husband. Every night in my home, as in most Irish homes, prayers went up for him, and for the President, and for all who were standing by the country. I have the greatest admiration for him, but this is not a matter of devotion to a leader, or devotion to a party, it is a matter of principle, and you may sneer at principle, some of you. It is a matter of conscience, a matter of right and wrong ... I cannot see what war has to do with it. You will say that is a woman's argument, but we know on whom the war comes hardest, and I repeat I don't see what war has to do with it. If we had not a soldier or a gun in the Irish Republican Army I would vote against that Treaty, and I will tell you why. I read and studied by myself the Terms of the Treaty when it was published..and, I admit and who could blame me, with a mind sharpened by sorrow, I came here for the last five days, and I listened to arguments which left my attitude unchanged. I am, as I said, a Separatist, and my objections to the Treaty are fundamental. This Treaty, which we are told gives us the substance of freedom, to my mind puts Ireland on a Dominion status within the British Empire. Now what have all these hundreds of years of struggle been for? What has it been about? What has been the agony and the sorrow for? Why was my husband murdered? Why am I a widow? Was it that I should come here and give my vote for a Treaty that puts Ireland within the British Empire ... Those who know me and my sorrow, if I may refer to that again, know what little bitterness I feel against the actual murderers of my husband. I can claim that they walked the streets of Limerick after he was shot, and I never asked, as I might have done, to have him avenged by Irish Republican Army bullets. But I do feel bitter now that the thing he and I cared about and worked for, the thing I lost my happiness for, should be voted away by young men, the young soldiers in whom we had such hope. He lies in Limerick in the Republican Plot, and though you Deputies of An Dáil bring Ireland within the Empire, there are points of it which your suffrages cannot touch. Where he lies is Republican ground, and I defy you to violate it. In this I speak for the other women who are careful for the honour of their dead. We are making history here today, and our decision will have a far-reaching effect. If there is any Deputy here who has not yet made up his mind, I would ask him for God's sake, before he does, to think well and stand for principle and against the Treaty.

Public Session, 20 December 1921

Mary MacSwiney

[England] has the military. I know that, but she cannot win this battle, for if she exterminates the men, the women will take their places, and, if she exterminates the women, the children are rising fast; and if she exterminates the men, women and children of this generation, the blades of grass, dyed with their blood, will rise, like the dragon's teeth of old, into armed men and the fight will begin in the next generation ... It is those who stand for the spiritual and the ideal that stand true and unflinching, and it is those who will win – not those who can inflict most but those who can endure most will conque ... The peoples of the world...know that peace can never be established except on the basis of truth and justice to all alike. Therefore our fight today has a chance of victory. You have told us it is between the acceptance of that document and war. I am not speaking as a young, ardent enthusiast. I am speaking as a woman who has thought and studied much, who realises, as only a woman can, the evils of war and the sufferings of war. Deputy Milroy yesterday in a speech to which I shall not allude, for it made me ashamed to think the public was listening to it, acknowledged that the women are the greatest sufferers of the war. I would ask him, if it were a democratic proposition, to let the women of Ireland judge this, and I have no doubt what the issue would be.

Public Session, 21 December 1921

Mrs Clarke

I rise to support the motion of the President to reject this Treaty. It is to me the simple question of right and wrong. To my mind it is a surrender of all our national ideals. I came to the first meeting of this session with this feeling strong upon me, and I have listened carefully to all the arguments in favour of the Treaty. But the only thing I can say of them is: maybe there is something in them; I can't see it. Arthur Griffith said he had brought back peace with England, and freedom to Ireland. I can only say it is not the kind of freedom I have looked forward to, and, if this Treaty is ratified, the result will be a divided people, the same old division will go on; those who will enter the British Empire and those who will not, and so England's old game of divide and conquer goes on. God, the tragedy of it! ... If England is powerful enough to impose on us Home Rule, Dominion or any other kind, let her do so, but in God's name do not accept or approve it – no more than you would any other Coercion Act. I heard big, strong, military men say here they would vote for this Treaty, which necessarily means taking an Oath of Allegiance, and I tell those men there is not power enough to force me, nor eloquence enough to influence me in the whole British Empire into taking that Oath, though I am only a frail scrap of humanity. I took an Oath to the Irish Republic, solemnly, reverently, meaning every word. I shall never go back from that. Like Deputy Duggan, I too can go back to 1916. Between 1 and 2 o'clock on the morning of May 3rd I, a prisoner in Dublin Castle, was roused from my rest on the floor, and taken under armed escort to Kilmainham Jail to see my husband for the last time. I saw him, not alone, but surrounded by British soldiers. He informed me he was to be shot at dawn. Was he in despair like the man who spoke of him on Tuesday? Not he. His head was up; his eyes flashing; his years seemed to have slipped from him; victory was in every line of him. 'Tell the Irish people,' he said, 'that I and my comrades believe we have saved the soul of Ireland. We believe she will never lie down again until she has gained absolute freedom.' And, though sorrow was in my heart, I gloried in him, and I have gloried in the men who have carried on the fight since; every one of them. I believe that even if they take a wrong turn now they will be brave enough to turn back when they discover it. I have sorrow in my heart now, but I don't despair; I never shall. I still believe in them.

Public Session, 22 December 1921

Countess Markievicz

I object to any government whereby a privileged number of classes established here by British rule are to be given a say ... in the form of an Upper Chamber, as against all, I might say, modern ideas of common sense, of the people who wish to build up a prosperous, contented nation. But looking as I do for the prosperity of the many, for the happiness and content of the workers, for what I stand, James Connolly's ideal of a Workers' Republic ...

A Deputy: A Soviet Republic!

Madame Markievicz – A co-operative commonwealth! – these men are to be set up to uphold English interests in Ireland, to uphold the capitalists' interests in Ireland, to block every ideal that the nation may wish to formulate ... I know what I mean – a state run by the Irish people for the people. That means a government that looks after the rights of the people before the rights of property. And under the Saorstat I don't wish to anticipate that the directors of this and that capitalist interest is to be at the head of it. My ideal is the Workers' Republic for which Connolly died. And I say that this is one of the things that England wishes to prevent. She would sooner give us Home Rule than a democratic Republic. It is the capitalists' interest in England and Ireland that are pushing this Treaty to block the march of the working people in Ireland and England ... But while Ireland is not free I remain a rebel, unconverted and unconvertible. I have seen the stars, and I am not going to follow a flickering will-o'-the-wisp.

Public Session, 3 January 1922

Mrs Pearse

It has been said here on several occasions that Padraig Pearse would have accepted this Treaty. I deny it. As his mother I deny it, and on his account I will not accept it. Neither would his brother Willie accept it, because his brother was part and parcel of him ... People will say to me 'The people of Ireland want this Treaty.' I have been through Ireland for the past few years and I know the hearts and sorrows of the wives of Ireland. I have studied them; no one studied them more, and let no one here say that these women from their hearts could say they accept that Treaty. They say it through fear; they say it through fear of the aeroplanes and all that has been said to them ... We will hold what they uphold, and no matter what anyone says I feel that I and others here have a right to speak in the name of their dead. (applause).

Public Session, 4 January 1922

Dr Ada English

THERE has been talk about compromise – that we compromised the position. I think that is a most unworthy thing to say. We had lots of things to bargain about – you had lots of material things to bargain about – questions of trade and commerce and finance and the use of ports; but nobody ever suspected we were going to compromise on the question of independence and the rights of the country. Mr MacGarry mentioned yesterday Land Acts taken in the past from England. There was no Republic in Ireland when we took the Land Acts from England. That makes a very great difference. And the Republic exists. You can take any Act you like that is consistent with the Republic, but you cannot take anything which gives away the Republic. It is not in your power to give it away. I have been asked by several people in the Dáil and elsewhere as to what views my constituents took about this matter. I credit my constituents with being honest people, just as honest as I consider myself – and I consider myself fairly honest – they sent me here as a Republican Deputy to An Dáil which is, I believe, the living Republican Parliament of this country. Not only that, but when I was selected as Deputy in this place I was very much surprised and, after I got out of jail, when I was well enough to see some of my constituents, I asked them how it came they selected me, and they told me they wanted someone they could depend on to stand fast by the Republic, and who would not let Galway down again (cheers). That is what my constituents told me they wanted when they sent me here, and they have got it (cheers)....

I think that it was a most brave thing today to listen to the speech by the Deputy from Sligo in reference to the women members of An Dáil, claiming that they only have the opinions they have because they have a grievance against England, or because their men folk were killed and murdered by England's representatives in this country. It was a most unworthy thing for any man to say here. I can say this more freely because, I thank my God, I have no dead men to throw in my teeth as a reason for holding the opinions I hold. I should like to say that I think it most unfair to the women Teachtai because Miss MacSwiney had suffered at England's hands. That, a Chinn Chomhairle is really all I want to say. I am against the Treaty, and I am very sorry to be opposition to (nodding towards Mr Griffith and Mr Collins). [Cheers]

Public Session, 4 January 1922

The Treaty was accepted by Dáil Eireann on 6 January with 64 votes in favour and 57 against.

DAIL EIREANN DEBATE ON IRISH WOMEN AND THE EXTENSION OF THE FRANCHISE: 2 MARCH 1922

Mrs O'Callaghan

I move 'That a decree be passed for its object the admission of Irish women to the Parliamentary Franchise on the same terms as Irish men.'...The women did their own part in the war during the last five years and I think they should be given the franchise now and I hope there is no Teachta here against it. The brave men who put their names to the proclamation of the Irish Republic in Easter Week wanted to put the men and women on the same footing on the voting register. I feel that I have not been treated fairly on this motion. This is the Bill which I now rise to propose.

REPRESENTATION OF THE PEOPLE BILL MEMORANDUM. – This Bill has for its object the admission of Irish women to the Parliamentary franchise on the same terms as Irish men.

I have the cause very much at heart. I was in a Suffrage Society ten years ago. It is not a measure or cause I am espousing today for Party purposes. The Bill, copies of which in English have been supplied to the members, has for its object the admission of these women for the first time as Irishwomen to the Parliamentary franchise. In other words, it is a Bill to enfranchise Irish women between the ages of 21 and 30 .... .I will confine myself to a statement of the general principle. The civilization of a country is marked by the position of its women and, by that test, Ireland stands high. The Proclamation of the Irish Republic in 1916 was addressed to Irishwomen as well as to Irishmen and guaranteed equal rights to all its citizens. It promised the people a national Government, elected by the suffrages of Irishmen and Irishwomen. I cannot believe that there is in this Parliament of the Irish Republic a single Deputy but holds with me that we ought now to remedy this injustice to a section of Irishwomen. During these last years of war and terror, these women in their twenties took their share in the dangers. They have purchased their right to the franchise and they have purchased their right to a say in this all-important question before the country. Without their votes or their voice, nobody can say that the will of the whole people of Ireland will have been ascertained.

Mr Griffith, President of the Republic, in reply to a women's deputation last week on the matter, while declaring his belief in equal suffrage for the sexes, put forward some objections. He said it was a mistake to say that the Dáil had the power to alter the Franchise. Since when has there been a limit to the power of the Dáil in Ireland? I understood that this was the sovereign authority in Ireland, deriving its power from the sovereign people. And I have yet to be convinced that that is not the case. The second objection he put forward was the difficulty of compiling the Register. I have no expert knowledge on this point but it seems to me absurd to say that it would require eight months. Three months is the time allowed for the general register to be compiled. Surely if this decree was passed by An Dáil, the work could be speeded up and brought into the time. The third objection is that if it were passed Great Britain would not recognise it and the fate of the Treaty would be affected, as President Griffith says. And when he says a thing I believe he believes it. But if President Griffith says that ninety-five per cent of the adult women voters of Ireland are solid for the Treaty there is his best argument in the world to make this Bill welcome across the water. I had hoped before the Session opened, when I was thinking of this, to get the support of many members of the Dáil for this measure, irrespective of Party. Now I am not so sure. However if any oppose it I only ask them one thing – not to accuse me of insincerity, of trailing a red herring, torpedoing the Treaty or anything like that. It is time I think in the Dáil that we tried to escape from the tyranny of the phrase. To cry 'red herring' at the measure does not in any way impair its nature or essential justice. I now propose this Bill and I ask the Dáil to pass it into law.

Madame de Markievicz

I rise to support this just measure for women because it is one of the things that I have worked for wherever I was since I was a young girl. My first realisation of tyranny came from some chance words spoken in favour of woman's suffrage and it raised a question of the tyranny it was intended to prevent – women voicing their opinions publicly in the ordinary and simple manner of registering their votes at the polling booth. That was my first bite, you may say, at the apple of freedom, and soon I got on to the other freedom, freedom to the nation, freedom to the workers. This question of votes for women, with the bigger thing, freedom for women and opening of the professions to women, has been one of the things that I have worked for and given my influence and time to procuring all my life whenever I got an opportunity. I have worked in Ireland, I have even worked in England, to help the women to obtain their freedom. I would work for it anywhere, as one of the crying wrongs of the world, that women, because of their sex, should be debarred from any position or any right that their brains entitle them a right to hold. In Ireland we have been in a rather difficult and complicated position. It has been the habit of our tyrants over in England to use Woman's Suffrage as a party cry. Each Party when it suited them ran the Suffrage Question for all it was worth. But when they were in a position to help the cause of Women Suffrage, the cry then was 'Oh! there is something more important before the nation.'

Now, I am sorry to accuse Mr Griffith of taking up that English attitude here in Ireland. Mr Griffith supported the Woman's Suffrage cause and he never varied when women suffragists were throwing axes at his political opponent, Mr Redmond.

Mr Griffith in those days spoke his opinions very freely as to woman's suffrage. In those days women felt that they did not want to seek representation at Westminster. I have a vote myself now to send men and women to the Dáil, and I wish to have that privilege extended to the young women of Ireland, whom I count in every way as my superiors. With the glorious innocence and intuition of youth they fixed their eyes on high ideals. They had the education that was denied to me in my youth and they have proved their valour during the years of the terror in a way that we, the older women, never got a chance to do. There was a dastardly remark about women in men's clothing made just now by the Teachta who spoke. I would challege the men of honour, the other men who did not even require women's clothes to get out of the way when shots were being fired, and I would ask would any man of the IRA turn down the girls who stood by the men in the days of the fight for freedom and did what the women did in the gap of danger? It is for these girls that I speak today and it is the experience that these girls had in the last year that has brought to birth in them a great desire for this small privilege – the right of citizenship in Ireland. Many years of organisation, of speechifying and talk did not enable our Franchise Society of noble women to put these ideals into the young women's hearts. But it is the work they have done during the last couple of years, where they have been dragged out of their shells and made to take their place as citizens at the polling booths, helping at the elections and helping the men on the run, that has put this desire into the hearts of the young women. This desire is voiced from every quarter in Ireland – this desire which I find re-echoing strongly in my heart. No one can say that with me it is a Party measure, for I have always done it, always pushed it and always tried to get the women their due and their rights. We have been in a difficult position in Ireland because we were on the run. When our Dáil was held in secret, it was impossible to bring forward measures like this. War measures were the only measures that were attended to and, naturally, the women did not push forward at the time when asking for their rights might have delayed people in a house where they would be in danger of murder. The women realised that, I realised that. I even wished to put this forward before in the Dáil, but there were so many difficulties in the Dáil – too many other subjects to be discussed – that I did not bring it forward. I have brought it forward before in different places. One Deputy here seems to think that Cumann na mBan would torpedo the Treaty. In the name of Cumann na mBan I thank him for his appreciation of their valour and strength and I can tell him that it will be up to them to do it whether they get the votes or not. Today, I would appeal here to the men of the IRA more than to any of the other men to see that justice is done to these young women and young girls who took a man's part in the Terror.

Mrs O'Callaghan
In winding up the case that has been made for the extension of the Franchise, I would like to stress the point that has been brought up by other speakers upon the necessity for a new register. I know what was done. I know what was done at Limerick. We have no new Register for the last period. We would be working on an out of date Register and it would be very unfair. Now as to the enfranchisement of women, I would really like if the Dáil could see its way to pass it. In the last resource, even if the Register would not be in time for the next election, I am very sure that the women who fought for the Republic and helped the Republic would like this measure to be passed by this Parliament of the Republic. I would appeal to you all on that ground. That is all I have got to say.

Miss MacSwiney
The motion that the question be now put was before you and you allowed two more speeches before deciding and now you have taken Mrs O'Callaghan's closing speech on the motion. It strikes me that the whole proceeding is out of order and that the motion is being most irregularly closed. [*The motion was lost: 38 votes in favour and 47 against.*]

Dáil Eireann, Official Report

AFTERMATH
We are all frightfully busy here, preparing for the elections. Though personally I should not be surprised if they were put off again. The Register is a farce. Griffith is afraid that if it is revised he will be beaten. None of the Volunteers are on. We brought in a Bill to enfranchise women under 30. Griffith turned it down. Quite spontaneously the demand arose here, women everywhere throughout the country suddenly finding their position to be humiliating, and it was the fight that did it. They say they must have a say as to the Treaty, and that if they are good enough to take part in the fight, they are good enough to vote.

Things are *awful* here. There are more people being killed weekly than before the truce.

Constance Markievicz to Eva Gore-Booth, c. July 1922.
Prison Letters of Constance Markievicz, p.298

PRELUDES TO WAR – WOMEN'S PEACE MISSIONS

A Pacifist Response

I have always been a Pacifist, and I was interested through the Women's International League for Peace and Freedom in efforts to avoid the Civil War. When the Republicans were in the Four Courts I was reproached – I had often been reproached by Francis Sheehy-Skeffington – that although I was a Pacifist working for peace, I didn't do much for peace in Ireland. When the Four Courts were attacked I felt the moment had come for some definite action on our part.

So I went round and saw AE and asked him was there anything to be done to stop the fighting. He was in a state of utter despair. He said there was nothing to be done and we would have to fight it out. Susan Mitchell was there. The two of us came out and sat on the stairs. She wept and wept over the whole thing.

I then went out to see one of our staff, Miss O'Connor, who lived in Rathmines. She said to me: 'There is one thing we can do; we can do something for the poor people who are living round the Four Courts. We can try to get them out of those houses.'

She and I and Miss Ryan started off and walked to Government Buildings and asked to see Mr Cosgrave. He saw us, and we waited in a large front office room. When he came in we were sitting in the middle of the room, and he said 'Oh, this is terrible,' and made us sit with our backs to the wall in case we might be fired on. We got a message round to all our friends to meet at the Mansion House the next day.

Among those who came were Mrs Sheehy-Skeffington, Maud Gonne MacBride, and Mrs Despard, and we were sent on as Peace emissaries to Government Buildings, where we saw Cosgrave, Griffith and Collins.

Collins was excited: obviously excited. Griffith was utterly depressed; an old, broken man. Cosgrave was outwardly unmoved, frigidly cold. After a lot of talk we saw that they were prepared, if the others would meet them, to try and negotiate. They didn't go very far, but they were prepared to talk, anyway. We went back: and then the difficulty was to get in touch with the republicans.

The Lord Mayor said that as the fighting was going on he would loan us the ambulance to cross town. It was the only way we could go to what used to be the tram parcels office, and which was now being used as some sort of headquarters for the IRA.

We went into some sort of dark room, with sacks all around it. I sat on a sack of flour or something. We couldn't see any of the Republicans, but eventually someone – a General-somebody-or-other, but I could never remember since who he was – had a long talk with Mrs Sheehy-Skeffington. But they would not negotiate on any terms.

They said they were into it now, and there was no way out but to fight it out.

Louie Bennett: *The People's Weekly*, 30 October 1948, quoted in R M Fox: *Louie Bennett,* pp. 76-8

Condemnation of the Provisional Government

GOVERNMENTIn June 1922, after the Pact had been made, I understood the two sections of the IRA had agreed not to fight each other, and I accepted a mission under Desmond Fitzgerald, Minister of Publicity, Provisional Government, to go to Paris to write up in the Press and make known abroad the fiendish murders of Catholics, especially Catholic children, which was being carried on by the Orangemen and Freemasons of Belfast ...

I was supplied with documents for this by a special bureau which existed at the time under the Provisional Government, in the basement of Government Buildings, Merrion Street, whose chief work it was to collect and classify Orange crimes.

Republicans and Free Staters agreed that a means must be found of stopping those crimes. It was with the approval of both sides that I went to Paris ...

On the morning of June 27, I read with amazement of the shelling of the Four Courts. Civil War was launched in Ireland. I rushed to the Irish Office so early that Colonel Moore received me in his dressing gown and showed me an official telegram he had received that night from the Provisional Government giving instructions to insist in the foreign press that the Irish Government was acting on its own and not on orders from England. I said I did not believe it. It seemed to me that Churchill's sudden determination to force Civil War in the South was the result of his fear of concerted action against the North (of which he may have got some inkling) rather than his indignation at the continued occupation of the Four Courts by the IRA, in spite of his and Lloyd George's speeches in the House of Commons on June 26 ...

I immediately left for Dublin. On arrival I went to the Lord Mayor, that man of peace, who has literally worn himself out in the cause. For the first time I saw him in despair. The shells were bursting over the Four Courts, every exit was surrounded, the place was filled with ammunition. At any moment one of the English shells might explode it, and the 400 IRA men inside would go up with it. They had refused to surrender. 'Get together some of the women who are not afraid and who want peace. We will make a supreme attempt.' I got Mrs Despard, Mrs Sheehy-Skeffington, Mrs Connery, Miss Jacob, the Misses Webb, Miss Connolly, Miss O'Connor, Mrs Johnson, Mrs O'Farrelly and Miss Louie Bennett.

The Lord Mayor telephoned that he was going with us into the Four Courts and asked that firing should cease while we were there.

As we descended the steps of the Mansion House a messenger arrived with the news that the surrender of the Four Courts had been ordered by the OC of the Republicans and the Dublin Brigade of the IRA, that the bombardment was to cease. 'Ladies' said the Lord Mayor, 'You were ready to risk your lives in the cause of Peace, I beg you will remain together as a committee to try and obtain it. A room in the Mansion House is at your disposal.' We all agreed, and the Women's Peace Committee was started. We arranged for two delegations – one to the Provisional Government, the other to the Republicans. We claimed, as women, on whom the misery of civil war would fall, that we had a right to be heard. We proposed an immediate cessation of hostilities till the meeting of An Dáil fixed for July 2, and that the question of civil war should be decided by the Parliament of the People, that during the truce all combatants should return to their homes, and that there should be no more arrests. One delegation, composed of Mrs Despard, Miss O'Farrelly, Miss Bennett, Miss Webb and myself were received by appointment at 12 o'clock on July 1 by Mr Griffith, Mr Collins and Mr Cosgrave in Government Buildings. The Government refused these conditions. The other delegation, consisting of Mrs Sheehy-Skeffington, Miss Bennett, Mrs Connery, Mrs Johnson, Miss Jacob, was received in the afternoon in the Hamman Hotel. The Republicans agreed to negotiate on these conditions, Mr Oscar Traynor remarking: 'We do not want to bring suffering and destruction on our fellow countrymen, we shall not fire a shot except in defence. We are willing to submit the question to the Dáil.'

In view of this statement and of the corroborating facts that both at the Four Courts and in O'Connell Street the Republicans to their own undoing, maintained a rigorously defensive attitude, what can one think of Mr Cosgrave's speech: 'At the Four Courts they should have knocked hell out of them,' and of the frequent taunts levelled by the Government Publicity Department at the Four Courts prisoners refusing to come out and fight. By remaining on the defensive the Republicans lost a military advantage, but they gained this, that in history the whole blame of the civil war will rest on the Free State ministers who, at Churchill's bidding, destroyed the Four Courts and O'Connell Street, and 'knocked hell' out of their former comrades on December 8, 1922, in Mountjoy prison yard, when they murdered Generals Rory O'Connor, Liam Mellows, Dick Barrett and Joe McKelvey.

Maud Gonne MacBride: *Eire*, 22 September 1923.

MANIFESTO FROM THE CONVENTION OF IRISH WOMEN WORKERS, HELD ON SUNDAY, 15 OCTOBER, 1922

We, women workers of Ireland, realizing that, so long as the country is devastated by civil strife, unemployment must persist and semi-starvation and other miseries become more acute for thousands of Irish people, call now upon both parties in the conflict to agree to an unconditional Truce as the first step towards a Peace Conference.

As helpless victims of the present unnatural strife,we claim our right to consideration from both parties and we believe that both must recognize the justice of such a claim.

Therefore we ask the Provisional Government and the Republican leaders publicly to proclaim their willingness to enter into a Truce and to take the necessary steps to realize it without delay.

We are sick of battles, and bloodshed and terror. We want Peace: we want work: we want security of Life and Home. We appeal to every member of the Dáil and to the rank and file of both Armies to back our claim for a restoration of these elementary rights through honourable negotiations.

R M Fox: *Louie Bennett*, pp.79-80

A JOURNEY TO DONEGAL

A week before the attack upon the Four Courts, Liam Mellows sent for me. He was staying at Mrs Woods' house in Donnybrook. He seemed to be in an unusually cheerful mood. Outlining to me how the two sides hoped to sink their differences through united action on the North, he explained that Mulcahy was acting on the F.S. side. Cumann na mBan was needed to set up a field hospital in Co. Donegal. He asked me to pick up six senior members of the organisation who would travel and set up the centre. He would have made all other necessary arrangements. They would be under the direct charge of Peadar O'Donnell's brother Frank, who would be travelling with them from Dublin by train, at 1.30 pm on Wednesday, 28th June. He emphasised the necessity of strict secrecy in case the proposal would be leaked, as the British Under Secretary was still in Phoenix Park. I immediately got in touch with Una O'Connor, Mary Cuddihy and Maire Comerford, and made arrangements with them. Liam promised each of us a small calibre revolver, which he duly delivered.

In addition to some first aid equipment which we packed, we also had cases of revolvers, ammunition and explosives.

On the evening of Tuesday 27th June, all of the Dublin IRA were mobilised. They were expecting the Staters to attack the Four Courts or other positions which the IRA. had taken over. They waited until about midnight, when they disbanded and went home. It was early on the following morning that I awoke to the noise of heavy guns by the army attacking the Four Courts ...

Emmet and I dressed quickly and after a rushed breakfast went off into the city. He went off to contact Mick Tannam of the 3rd Battalion. I went on in as far as Parnell Square to try to contact somebody. I eventually met Maire Comerford on her bicycle and we discussed what we should do about the journey to the North. Were the two sides really locked in combat and had it all fallen apart? Maire said she would try to get into the Four Courts and find out. Off she went, to return after some time to say she got into the Four Courts and despite concentrated shell fire and rifle fire was told that the arrangements about the North still held and they were to proceed up there as arranged. This surprised me; perhaps it was just a localised conflict after all. It was now after 11.30, and I had to rush home to Donnybrook to collect a few things and hurry back to the station for the 1.30 train ...

After an uneventful journey, we reached Sligo and went to the barracks which were occupied by Republican IRA under Brian MacNeill. Liam Pilkington, who was in command of the 3rd Western Division, was also there. He arranged for a car to bring us to Ballybofey, where the centre was being set up. The car was well crowded with the Cumann na mBan girls, Frank O'Donnell and local IRA boys. We got as far as Finner camp where we remained for the night. Next morning we drove on to Ballybofey, and found the headquarters. There we were told that the armaments we had brought from Dublin were not needed; they had more than enough themselves and that they might be required more urgently in Dublin. Apparently the Cumann na mBan team were not needed either, so we all retraced our steps back to Finner camp. On the way there I got one of the IRA men to sing some Donegal songs for us. He did so, in a hauntingly beautiful voice. We all fell silent, each one I suppose thinking different thoughts ...

It was evening when we got to Finner and the garrison did their best to get us to remain for the night. Frank O'Donnell wisely said he would not; that he must see the girls were in a safe area. He endeavoured to get the garrison to abandon the camp. The Commandant however said that everything would be alright – that there was no tension or disagreement between the two sides so far north as Co. Donegal. I said I did not like to interfere but for once I made an impassioned plea for the garrison to get out – that the place could not be defended, it was so open. All to no avail ... Eventually with Frank we drove on to Bundoran. It was now quite late at night and we were all dead tired, so we went to bed and fell fast asleep.

Moments later it seemed, in the dead of night, there was heavy knocking at my door. It was Frank O'Donnell shouting that Finner Camp had been attacked and taken by the Staters. The young IRA boy, Jim Connolly of Kinlough, who had sung for us all in the car earlier in the afternoon, had been shot dead. They'd better get out as fast as possible to a safe house which he knew and which was about two miles outside Bundoran, on the Sligo road. I dressed as quickly as possible, picked up some of the heavy cases containing the guns etc., and, with the other girls accompanied by Frank, with a rifle slung over his shoulder, started walking along the deserted street and out the country road until we reached the safe cottage. Here we all stayed sitting around the open turf fire until early morning when the people of the cottage knew of a van which went into Sligo every morning. We were given a lift on this and arrived safely back at the barracks.

Sighle Bean Uí Dhonnchadha (Sheila Humphreys O'Donoghue),
Uinseann Mac Eoin (ed.): *Survivors*, pp. 342-4

IN THE FOUR COURTS

Liam, looking very determined, called Bridie Clyne and I into a great big room where there were two beds in the inside corner, and told us to go to sleep. He forbade us from leaving that corner of the room because the rest of it was dangerous. The moon gave light enough to show fragments of glass which were hanging from the tall window. I was still too excited and angry to sleep. But I lay there obediently and watched Liam's small figure as, ignoring the other noises, he moved about on tip toe. He changed the position of a table, and other things, to bring all the amenities he could provide for us into the safety zone. If anybody came to the door he behaved like a nurse in a sick room, shooing them away.

But a moment came when he was not on the spot. Then the door flew open before Sean Nolan's shoulder, and he made straight for our corner, obviously coming off duty and expecting a bed. He didn't see us. He humped his rifle on top of me and sat down heavily on Bridie. After that Liam gave up and we talked the night away.

Outside, on a marble floor, under a marble pillar, I saw Rory O'Connor; he was curled up and fast asleep. It was not hard to guess who should have been in one of the beds given over to us.

There was a job outside for me first thing in the morning, but when I wheeled my bike to the guardroom door I found the whole floor full of men asleep, in every kind of attitude; some on top of the others. The sun was coming through a deep and narrow hole where a shell had taken part of the corner of the building, without bursting. Liam took my bicycle and told me to follow him. He held it high over his head and we walked across the room of bodies to the side exit.

On the second day there was a stir of preparation and I saw the men preparing to go out. Imitating them I packed my pockets, and tied things, I don't remember what, on to my belt. Obviously one should keep one's hands free. I broke our parcels of bandages and divided them between the men. I remember handing Ginger his share, and the dumb look he gave me.

I know now that Ernie O'Malley was to lead the break-out, which did not come off. By then, to emerge would have been suicide. Only the Fire Brigade could, and did, come, several times.

Nobody called off the operation, and I do not know when it was abandoned. Our belts were closed and coats still buttoned as night fell. I remember leaning against sacks in a small place which was crowded, and that George Plunkett several times came over to tuck a coat, his own, around my legs.

At 3 am that morning Madge was still doing her rounds, with her bucket of tea and dry bread, which she had made and baked in one of the ovens in the Courts. She told me 'I found Liam standing on guard over his men while they slept – had his rifle in his hand – certainly looking very sad. That was, I'm sure, the last 'bit' he had until he reached the Joy.'

She gripped the back of a balcony, or circular seating, and I had my head as low as it would go between my arms, and so stood all, or most of the volunteers, with backs to the wall in the centre of the Four Courts. The leaders had arranged us there, and they were in a mood that answered no questions, and invited no argument. The orders, sterner than I had heard before, or since, held us in position. There was no announcement, that I recall, that the big explosion was coming; but nobody can have been in much doubt.

The shock blew me back, the full length of my arms, then forward again, while dust and fragments scattered everywhere, including something light that slid down my back. As far as I know Paddy O'Brien was the only man on our side hurt; obviously he had been minding us so well he did not mind himself enough.

After the explosion we were all crowded together, near the eastern side gate. The Fire Brigade came to take Paddy O'Brien, and perhaps other wounded if they had not already gone. We had to squash together in a ring around the argument between Paddy and the others. He did not want to go. Eventually he said that he was OC and no one there could give him orders. But Liam (I think) told him that because he was wounded and unable to command any further, he had been replaced; he must accept the decision to send him out. It was an order.

It could not have been a more distressful, affectionate parting if Rory and Liam and Dick, and Joe and Paddy had known at the time that they would not meet again in this life.

So the Fire Brigade took Paddy out. Presently he escaped from hospital, only to bleed slowly to death, from a sniper's bullet, in Enniscorthy.

Now was the time of surrender. Father Albert put a Red Cross band on my arm. But I had not been all the time on Red Cross duty, so I had a scruple. It was not a suitable time to show false colours, so I tore it off, and marched out with the men, wheeling my bicycle. Lorries were waiting for us on Bachelors Walk, but I managed not to go.

Máire Comerford, *Autobiography*

WAR IN DUBLIN

After that we began to slip rapidly into civil war. The Four Courts was occupied in April, and I was often in and out of them. Liam (Mellows) and I continued to be close friends. He seemed to think that I could give him a fresh slant on events. One day he brought forth a tricolour flag. It had rested upon the coffin of one of our heroes. *Keep that*, Nora, he said. *You may yet need to place it on the grave of another Republican.*

Seamus and I had been married some months when the outbreak occurred on June 28th, 1922. We had slept that night at Margaret Skinnider's and were awakened by the boom of artillery. Quickly we hurried from Fairview to Barry's Hotel, which was a Republican headquarters. There was confusion everywhere. I was sent in charge of medicines to Tara Hall, which was in Talbot Street, while Seamus was directed to go to a post in the Gresham. I sent squads scouring the chemist shops for the medicines we needed. We did not always get co-operation. A change that was plain to see had come over the business community. Aghna, however, had done a course as a midwife and she was now helping us. She went with the squads because she could identify upon the shelves just what was needed and they could not fool her. Everything was in large glass jars at that time. She would point at one; take that. We got well stocked up with supplies. We had a first-aid post at Tara Hall, though we did not have many to heal there. One night, however, Free State soldiers came with one of their men for treatment, and of course he was treated.

One day I went to the Gresham, which was now being bombarded. I entered by a door and followed through holes in walls, until I came to a room where they hoped to have a first-aid post. But we had not the time or the personnel to set it up. I returned to Tara Hall. We had no beds there; we simply lay at night upon the stage with coats thrown over us.

We were there scarcely a week, when all the posts on the east side of O'Connell Street were over-run and we had to evacuate. I did not know where Seamus was. We had parted at Barry's a week before. For all I knew, he could be wounded or dead.

I left then, on the run now, to take up a post with our shadow headquarters. Austin Stack was in charge of finance. Margaret Skinnider had gone as his secretary but was arrested shortly afterwards. I stepped into the gap. Seamus, meanwhile, had turned up safely. We found a flat upon the top floor of Craobh na gCuig Cuigi, on the corner of Hume Street and Ely Place. I was there only a few weeks when we were raided. I had just completed copying records for Stack, and had got them safely to him, when the Intelligence Squad from Oriel House arrived. They searched our place high up and low down, but although we had some very important documents, including a money draft for £5,000 which I would have hated them to find, they came upon nothing except a ninepenny receipt for one of our fund raisers. That was the sole evidence they had against me.

You had better get ready and come with us. We were brought to Portobello Barracks, which had a sinister reputation. We were held there a day, but at the end of it they came in and said to me: *You will go to Mountjoy.* It showed me what the new state thought of the children of 1916. *And you,* they turned to Seamus, *how would you like to go there too? Oh, be God, I would.* They called a taxi and we both went together to the Joy, parting at the gate, he into one prison and I into another. It was November, 1922, and we were to spend our first anniversary in jail.

Nora Connolly O'Brien, Uinseann Mac Eoin
(ed.): *Survivors*, pp. 211-2

MORAN'S HOTEL

I was transferred to the Dublin Central Branch, and attended the meetings in Parnell Square, again giving lectures and demonstrations on dressings and bandaging. Then, when Civil War broke out, there came a message for me to go to Barry's Hotel, and report there for duty. But I was only a few hours there when a man arrived in a car to take me to Moran's Hotel, in Gardiner Street, and there we drove like lightning, speeding though the streets in a flash.

We nurses and the Cumann na mBan occupied the big basement of the hotel, using a large kitchen for the cooking, and several smaller rooms for dressings and other needs. We did not take off our clothes during those days, lying down for a few hours now and then, but sleep was well nigh impossible with the constant firing going on ... We were in Moran's Hotel until the Sunday afternoon, only four days, but they might be four months, so well do I remember them ...

The men were splendid, with always the joke and the laugh in spite of the hard time they went through. Each morning, those of them who were detailed for commissariat duty, would come to ask what we were in need of in the way of stores. Then they would sally forth and return with what we needed, which they had obtained by the simple expedient of holding up the bread cart and taking what bread we wanted, and the same with the milkman. They also got other food as well, we were never short of anything, and there had been a good supply of tea and sugar and such like in the hotel ...

On the Sunday afternoon we were given the order to evacuate Moran's and make our way – by the tunnels which our engineers had made in the walls – higher up the street. But first there was the land mine which our men had decided to let off the last thing before leaving the place. I have never been able to know why this was done, but Tom Irwin has told me that it was to make matters more difficult for the enemy. We, who were Red Cross workers, decided to remain until this was done; there might be someone hurt and perhaps left behind ... We tried to pray, someone started the Rosary. I sat on the floor, with my precious First Aid dressings to which I clung frantically, determined not to part with it if possible ... At last, a rumble, increasing to a roar, and we knew the mine had gone off. The walls shook, we were almost covered with dust and whitewash, but – we were alive. When we had got our breath again, we struggled to our feet and made our way to some area steps and so into the blinding light of the summer afternoon ...

[After some time in the Gresham Hotel with de Valera's forces –]
We went out into the night, and during the following hours we found shelter in two places – in a house in North Great George's Street, and in the Protestant Church of St. Thomas ... I think that the church was the last place we were in, for it was just daylight when we left to try and make our way to our various homes. As we left the church we passed Cathal Brugha at the door. What he was doing there I do not know, he may have come to give the order that we were to leave, but it was the last time I was to see him alive. We met Madame Markievicz just outside, she wanted to go inside where she had left her revolver.

I made my way back to Gardiner Place fairly easily, but some of the others had longer and far more difficult journeys to make.

Yet, when at last I was in bed, sleep would not come to me for a long time, so unhappy, so wretched did I feel. The firing, too, was so loud that it might have almost been in the same room with me.

Annie M P Smithson: *Myself – And Others*, pp. 250-9

BURYING THE DEAD

Mrs Cathal Brugha requests that, apart from family relations and intimate friends, the chief mourners and the Guard of Honour should include only the women of the Republican Movement. She makes this request as a protest against the 'immediate and terrible' Civil War made by the so-called Provisional Government on the Irish Republican forces.

She does not desire the presence of any of the representatives of the Free State or its officials at the Funeral.

NOTE – This does not exclude the general public from attending the funeral.

Sinn Féin Publicity Department, 9 July 1922.
National Library of Ireland

CHAPTER 8

Prison Experiences

Between the years 1916 and 1923, significant numbers of women were imprisoned. Many of the women were relatives of male leaders and regarded their role as one of upholding – whatever the cost – the principles that their men had died for. They wanted no special treatment because of their sex, arguing that equality in status with their male comrades should be maintained even in imprisonment.

HOLLOWAY 1918
Constance Markievicz, Maud Gonne MacBride and Kathleen Clarke were held together in Holloway Jail during the 'German Plot' arrests of 1918. Kathleen Clarke's account portrays the personal anguish suffered, as well as the resolute determination to continue resistance to every aspect of British rule over Irish people.

When the officials had received orders to prepare for the reception of rebel Irish women, they must have thought it was wild animals they would have to deal with. All one side of what was called the 'Hard Nails Wing' of the jail was cleared of all other prisoners, and between each of our cells there were three empty ones. The cells were furnished with a camp bed without springs, just iron slats with hills and hollows, and a mattress that seemed made of hay. After a short time lying on it, the hills worked their way up, and poor sleepers like myself spent the night trying to dodge those hills. The pillow was another sort of torment; I don't know what it was filled with, but it was so hard the head made no impression on it. Then the blankets were so hard and stiff that all efforts to snuggle into them for warmth or comfort were unavailing, and the sheets were thick, coarse and hard. These things, which were such a source of discomfort to me, had no effect on Madame Markievicz. She said she could sleep on stones, and Madame MacBride made no complaint.

The first month in prison I lost nine pounds in weight. At the time I could not afford to lose one pound, I was so light. I had no news of my children, where they were or what had happened to them after I had left them in Richmond Avenue, and for six weeks I was kept in this state of suspense, as up to then we were not allowed to write or receive letters. If I had been told that the rug the soldier put over me in the boat had come from my sister, I would have known their aunts had arrived in Dublin and that the children would be all right, and I would have been spared the awful weeks of suspense...

I had one great trouble all through my imprisonment, I could not sleep. Hour after hour went by each night, but no sleep. The doctor offered to give me things to make me sleep, but I was afraid of them, and refused. My imagination worked overtime during those long, dark, sleepless nights; I pictured countless dangers for my children, and went from that to my husband and all he had suffered during those terrible years in prison. Memories of Kilmainham came alive, and from that my mind went to the prison yard where I pictured him shot, not dead, but wounded to death and left to die slowly, in agony, or else finished off by an officer with a pistol. A story had circulated after the Rising that one of the executed men had met with that fate, and I always feared it had been he. Lying awake in the dark, from 8 pm until seven o'clock in the morning, there was nothing too awful for me to imagine. During the day, I could find occupation for my mind, and keep these thoughts at bay, but it was always a maddening thought that no matter what happened to my children, I could not go to them ...

Madame and I were very glad when Madame MacBride was released (October 1918). Imprisonment had a very depressing effect on her, and was undermining her health. All through her imprisonment she was kind, gentle and very courteous; she had very charming manners. I missed her, but was glad she was out of it. When she had gone some days, the doctor came to me and asked me to make an appeal for release on the grounds of health, as I was a good subject for release on such grounds, much better than Madame MacBride. He said that if I would appeal, he would have me released in a week. I refused, saying that I would never appeal to the British government for anything; when I left the prison, it would not be as the result of an appeal from me. He looked at me as if he could not understand me, and walked off without another word. I think I bewildered him many times.

(Helen Litton (ed): *Revolutionary Woman: Kathleen Clarke*, pp. 156-7, 161

AFTER RELEASE
My dear Mrs Skeffington

It is such a joy to be out of that awful place Holloway and to see Seagan and Iseult, but it is a heartbreak to leave Constance

Markievicz and Kathleen Clarke still ... up there. They are so brave and so uncomplaining and so willing to suffer for Ireland.

I hope that Con is elected to parliament. She would be a splendid candidate on social and labour questions as well as the national question.

On my release from jail I was driven to Seagan and Iseult's – who had to sign a paper taking me into her care. Saw Mr King. Still weak and in bed, only sitting up for a few hours.

P.S. Just seen by Independent your election on executive. So glad.

Maud Gonne MacBride, November 1918: *Sheehy-Skeffington Papers*
MS 24,106. National Library of Ireland

My dear Hanna

Saw Doctor who said both my lungs were affected and need treatment and great quiet and advised me to go to Ireland where I would be under Dr ... who was treating me before my arrest and also that in Ireland I would get more butter and cream than in England. Left the nursing home last Monday and since then three or four detectives have been planted outside the door and follow me. At the passport office where I went for a passport to Ireland I was told the authorities have not made up their minds what they are going to do with me yet.

[*Received a letter from Yeats*] ... who was told by the authorities I had left the nursing home and if his friend had died in which sanitorium she was to be interned ... but my mind is quite made up, I will go to no sanitorium in England, instead coming home and if put back in Holloway shall hunger strike at once ... what devils English officials are!

Maud Gonne MacBride, n.d. (1918): *Sheehy-Skeffington Papers*, MS
24,111. National Library of Ireland

A PRISONER ALONE
Constance Markievicz was eventually the only Irish prisoner left in Holloway. In a cheerful letter to her sister, Eva Gore-Booth, she reassured Eva that she was fine, continued to show anxiety about Kathleen Clarke, and discussed the 1918 election.

Here I am, all alone, in this Englishwoman's home! Luckily, I always find myself in good company. Of course, I miss K. very much, but for the first time in my life I was thankful to see the back of a dear friend.

Give her a good 'scholding' and a hug from me and tell her the tea-pot's broken, but *not* by me this time! I've no one to bully now, and she needs it. Tell her to stay in bed or rest up. Weren't you shocked when you saw her? and they dare to talk about German atrocities, the hypocrites! But it will all react in the end...

It wasn't talk blocked conscription: it was the astounding fact that the whole male population left at home and most of the women and kids would have died rather than fight for England, and they simply dare not exterminate a nation.

Our contempt of money and our taking death and jails as all in the day's work must puzzle the British more than a little.

You criticise our election organisation! The enemy says it was 'efficient', 'perfect,' etc. It was practically nil!

So everyone butted in, women and children taking a very promi-nent part.

I believe it brought out a lot of women speakers.

Constance de Markievicz to Eva Gore-Booth, 14 February 1919:
Prison Letters of Constance Markievicz, pp. 194-5

NO SPECIAL TREATMENT

As Hanna Sheehy-Skeffington had been imprisoned in Holloway for a few days in 1918 she had first-hand evidence of the state of health of the other women and was anxious to mount a campaign on their behalf. However, Mrs Wyse-Power's letter made it clear that such a campaign would be rejected by the women.

Surely you do not think that Cumann na mBan wants any incentive to urge them to agitate for the release of Madam. Perhaps Madam's own letter which I enclose for your consideration will show you that she wishes at all events consultation before she is detached from the other prisoners in any effort to obtain her release. This I know for a very long time and after my crossing with Mrs Clarke I realized fully that neither of them wished any special efforts made on their behalf as women. And resented keenly any special reference to them as apart from the men. Whether we think this judgement is right or not, at all events we have got to abide by it ...

Jenny Wyse-Power to Hanna Sheehy-Skeffington, 1 March 1919:
Sheehy-Skeffington Papers MS 22,689. National Library of Ireland

This attitude was referred to again shortly before the Truce, when Hanna Sheehy-Skeffington was in correspondence with Eva Gore-Booth while trying to ensure that Constance Markievicz, now Minister for Labour, would be released along with other prominent Sinn Féin leaders.

I rang up press and Castle and prison. No news. But apparently it was they thought C. might be out shortly. Since then nothing. Position briefly this. Dev and Grif. are not asking any releases – didn't ask G's or Bartons. These 'happened' just. G and McM were unsentenced and two others Dáil members were released with these – apparently under mistaken notion that these were Cab. ministers. They aren't. Duggan and Staines (latter IRA). Then we thought no sentenced MPs would be let out when to our surprise Barton was. He only got 1/2 hour notice. Now as far as I know Con is the only minister in, but the govt. may not even know this as they are stupid. Any other Mins. I know are 'on the run' – Stack, Blythe, Cosgrave, Collins. Con was seen last Sat by Miss Gifford ('John Brennan' y know) who went in as 'typist' with solicitor (Noyk) to witness her will. (This was commonplace) now Miss G. reports her anxious to get out and very eager about it, hoping for news. She (Con) didn't know that no one was being asked for and hoped Dev or Mick would move. As Lab. Min. she wants to be there at any conference ... Now my personal opinion is that Barton's relatives put pressure on unofficially – else why select him? He got 5 and she only 2 years – and so I'd say send letters to press just pointing out that Cab. Min. for Labour is still locked up, get questions in Parliament – all done individually. She said perhaps their women would but when our League tried that before, you know, we were snubbed by C. herself and told to stop! So it makes it difficult especially as I think if she knew these other details that she mightn't care for any society to move. And besides I don't know how you feel – myself I'd say get her out because its her desire to be out and if B. and rest are out why keep her in? But I know she hates being treated as a woman so it ought to be as 'Lab. Min.' I also hear your family (Sligo) doesn't want her out but not for your reason – again of course I can't say if this is true. Anyhow if not out soon it may be too late. She is reported thin and rather nervously excited, inclined to fidget etc though of course not ill. But naturally she must be straining at the leash just now.

I give you details and leave it with you to take any action. Let me know if I can help in any way ...

Hanna Sheehy-Skeffington to Eva Gore-Booth, 1920:
Eva Gore-Booth Papers, MS 21,816. National Library of Ireland

ESCAPE – TWO TALES

Mountjoy

One notable escape, that of three very prominent Cumann na mBan women from Mountjoy jail during the War of Independence, has entered the annals of Irish republican prison exploits. Although similar to male accounts of such escapades, it also possesses a specifically gendered quality.

Now, the first idea of escaping at all came to me from one of the male political prisoners. The hospital windows overlooked the ground where the 'murder gang' as they were called, assembled for exercise, and I found that one of the windows in the corridor could be raised three or four inches from the bottom, and it was lowered more than half-an-inch from the top; and it was in this way that I got into communication with a friend of mine who was doing twenty years. His first salutation to me when he knew I was there was: 'Up, Sligo!' Another male prisoner, under sentence of death, used to attend the hospital to have a wound dressed, and he brought notes which he gave to a hospital political prisoner on exercise just underneath our window. A stone and a good aim did the rest, and I got a regular mail! The notes were written to keep up my heart, and were full of humour and very amusing; I have them still as a souvenir of that time.

It was this correspondent who gave me the first idea of trying to escape, for which I have to thank him. Now that it is all over, I can say that I think I spoiled a stunt of his own which was coming off at the same time; but such are the fortunes of war, and he was very anxious that we should not put off our attempt, as he knew our plans, and approved of them. We were not sure till the very last minute that we would be able to manage, and we were terribly excited and anxious. The three others besides myself who decided to risk it were [Aileen] Keogh, Mary Bourke, and Eithne Coyle. Three others who were very young remained behind, none of us would take the responsibility of bringing them with us or letting them take such a risk.

I was in the hospital at the time and the other three in the prison. They had considered during the previous week the advisability of creating an atmosphere of noise or quiet during the hour fixed for our escape – 7 p.m. At first they tried quietness at that hour every night, and found that when they were very quiet – presumably studying – the wardresses came very frequently to see them. Then they tried being very noisy at that hour, and played football and danced Irish reels in the corridors, and found that while the noise continued the wardresses did not come up so often.

I was presently transferred from the hospital to the prison, and we used to play these games and make plenty of noise every evening at the same hour. The three girls who were not coming with us used to join in the games, too. On the fateful evening we were playing a game of football – Cork v. the Rest of Ireland; we were very noisy, and I must confess rather more excited than the game warranted as the hour of seven o'clock drew near!

Ten minutes before the hour one of us slipped away, and we others followed at intervals of a few moments each. I was the last to leave, and as I departed I got a good kick at the ball and gained a goal for the Rest of Ireland. I shouted 'Up, Sligo!' and those were my last words within the walls of Mountjoy. As I left I carefully locked the corridor doors with my duplicate keys; the three girls left behind kept up the noise on purpose, and we heard afterwards that it was almost two hours later before our escape was discovered. Those of us who were making our desperate bid for freedom met outside, and a few minutes later we thought all was lost! The door of the officers' quarters opened, and two wardresses came out, and passed close to where we stood flattened against the wall of the building, so close that I thought they must hear our very breathing and the thumping of our hearts! But they were chatting amongst themselves, and passed us by. If they had but guessed I wouldn't be telling this story now!

At the arranged spot a small scent bottle was thrown – the pre-arranged signal – and the next moment the rope ladder came dangling over the wall, the wall that was 25 feet high! I took it and pulled it; the wall at the top is flat and square, and the rope caught and was torn! Again we thought we were lost, but it was fixed for us, and flung over again, and this time I pulled it carefully down, and then began to climb. Oh! the swaying and the swinging of that rope ladder! I often wonder now how I ever reached the top. But when I *did* reach the top, and sat on the wall for a minute and looked down at the 25 feet on the other downward side, and saw my three friends who were waiting for us, looking like little pigmies in the distance, well, I can never think how I ventured down the knotted rope which was on that side. I heard the voice of my friend who had met me at Dun Laoghaire, saying:

'Slither, Linda; *slither!*'

And I slithered – to freedom!

The others followed, and once outside the grey walls of the prison we divided in pairs. Mary Bourke (who was doing two years hard labour) and myself went together, and drifted away in the kindly gloom, and we could only clasp each other's hands and whisper again and yet again, 'Is it true? Are we really free!'

We shared the same room that night in a friend's house, and how delightful everything seemed. She had a visitor in her spare bedroom, but that visitor insisted on giving us the room; and oh! the cool, clean linen, the eiderdown, even the very wallpaper, and then the dainty supper table and such glorious coffee! – all were a pleasure untold to our poor, starved senses, sick and weary of the eternal greyness of prison walls and days. How we talked that night! going over every detail of our escape, and laughing heartily over some of them. Of luggage we had none: I came away with a nail file and a fountain pen! But this mattered, indeed, little in comparison with the stupendous fact that we were once more free, even although that freedom had its limitations.

Annie M P Smithson (ed.): *In Times of Peril: Leaves from the Diary of Nurse Linda Kearns from Easter Week, 1916 to Mountjoy*, pp. 54-57

Kilmainham

During the Civil War women in 'B' Wing in Kilmainham decided to attempt to dig a tunnel in an old laundry room situated at the side of the exercise yard of the wing. Work continued for almost a month before the matron questioned Margaret Buckley about 'the hole in the laundry'.

This was the unkindest cut of all: our first-born, beautiful tunnel, the channel of escape, navigated and excavated by our own hands, those hands, the broken finger-nails of which bore silent but eloquent witness to the magnitude of the work undertaken; the passage to freedom, paved with the hopes and aspirations of a score of liberty-loving women; the altar on which we placed our prayers and our back-breaking adventure; and now, a blue-robed philistine dubs it 'the hole in the laundry' ... I, in silence, followed her to the top of the small opening, at the end of the corridor, which looked like a trap, without a door, guarded by iron bars. She pointed to it, and said what I already knew: 'That is how they got into the laundry; do you think that you could get down?'

'Getting down' meant taking hold of the iron bars, and swinging oneself (Blarney Castle wise) into the aperature, and then dropping to terra firma.

As I had never been down, and was no feather-weight, I was a bit nervous of 'the drop', but I looked her steadily in the eye, and replied: 'If you can get down there, I can.'

So she went first, and I followed, and to say that what I saw amazed me is a mild way of putting it. I gazed with wonder and admiration at a long gaping grave, nearly the length of the room in which we stood, which meant nearly half the width of the yard, and deep enough to reach my waist when I stood into it. There was no sign of the clay which had been dug out: it had been carted into an alcove behind, so as to be out of sight, and this, in itself, was no easy job. The hole was covered up each night so that a casual inspection would reveal nothing.

And still I gazed, and still I wondered how those girls, with no tools, with bare hands, and strength of purpose, could accomplish so much ... how dared she, or anyone, belittle their gigantic efforts. This was no 'hole in the laundry': this was a splendid achievement, the beginning of a real live tunnel, of which no man might be ashamed; and this was accomplished by the women and girls of B Wing, who had done me the honour of electing me their O.C. Once again, I thanked God for them, and sorrow filled my heart when I remembered that I had to tell them of this heart-breaking discovery ... I might have known that they would take it bravely. Sighle murmured: 'Go bhoiridh Dia orainn'; Judy took a fit of laughing; and May Connolly said: 'Better luck next time.'

That is the spirit of the Gael, and the women of Ireland are saturated with it; that is the spirit which kept the eyes of the mother of Kevin Barry fixed on the Tabernacle, in a nearby church, while the hangman's rope was being fastened about the neck of her boy; that is the spirit which upheld the sisters of Terence MacSwiney as they shared his agony in Brixton jail; that is the spirit which animates the wife of Cathal Brugha, who lives to instil into her children the 'NO SURRENDER' policy of their indomitable father.

The matter of the tunnel was a small thing, perhaps, but 'a straw shows how the wind blows.'

Margaret Buckley: *The Jangle of the Keys*, pp. 90-4

EASTER WEEK IN KILMAINHAM 1923
Almost four hundred women were jailed during the Civil War period. For a small group of women, imprisonment had become a family tradition they were proud to uphold.

We were not altogether unfortunate to be in this prison on April 24. It was a good place and day to take again – some of us for the first time – the Oath of Allegiance to the Republic. It was good to be prisoners, and to know that it was because we had been faithful to their dead and would not waste their sacrifice that we were here. Even the agony of watching the long hunger strike of some of the women we love and honour most became, yesterday, easier to bear. In the morning there was a requiem mass, in the afternoon the prisoners – nearly 300 – went in procession to the place of the executions and said the rosary

143

there. In front marched the women of Easter Week – Mrs Humphries and Miss O'Rahilly, Nora Connolly, Lily O'Brennan, Grace Plunkett and others; it was Grace Plunkett who laid our laurel wreath on the stone.

In the prison compound then Mrs Plunkett unfurled the tricolour, while 'Faith of our Fathers' was sung by all the prisoners. Then Lily O'Brennan spoke in Irish, and afterwards in English on 'Kilmainham in 1916' and the life and death of Eamon Ceannt; a paper on 'Joseph Plunkett' by Mrs Plunkett was read – a paper that made us realise again how wide and deep and high was the thought for which he and his great comrades lived and died. Then Nora Connolly spoke. She read the Proclamation of the Republic and James Connolly's last statement – it was as if the voices of our dead leaders were speaking to us again – no one who was here will forget. Then we took the Republican oath.

It was a day full of great sorrow – sorrow to have lost those leaders whose heroic, gentle spirits seemed so near us, so much to be loved, heavy sorrow that their own countrymen have betrayed them and desecrated their place of martyrdom, but it was a sorrow full of pride, full of hope – a sacrament of confirmation in the Republican faith. We are glad to have been here.

Dorothy Macardle: *Eire*, 12 May 1923

THE NORTH DUBLIN UNION RIOT

Eighty-one women in Kilmainham refused to allow themselves to be removed to the North Dublin Union, site of a former workhouse, because of their concern over two of the prisoners who were on hunger strike, a weapon frequently resorted to at this time. An infamous riot was the outcome.

It was the nineteenth day of their hunger strike. Mrs O'Callaghan was suffering a great deal, and we were very anxious about Miss MacSwiney. She seemed much weaker than on her last day in Mountjoy, restless, troubled by heart attacks and sudden alarming collapses. We knew the doctor had made an urgent report and hoped, every time the gate opened, to see two stretcher-bearers coming in.

At about 3 o'clock word came from the Governor that we were to be removed to the North Dublin Union that night. A meeting of the prisoners was immediately summonsed, it was unanimous. To leave the hunger strikers alone in the empty jail, at the mercy of such cruel tricks as were played on Miss Costello, was unthinkable. We sent our decision to the Governor at 4 o'clock; no prisoner would consent to leave until the hunger strikers were released. We expected their release at any moment and we went to our cells to pack. It was about 9 o'clock when the Governor, Begley, sent again to say that 81 prisoners were to be removed, if necessary by force. When asked whether woman-beating was a soldier's work he replied, 'I don't mind that. I have beaten my wife.' We prepared our plan of resistance. Suddenly a rumour flew through the prison; stretcher-bearers had come in: then a moment of joyous triumph and a shock of dismay – Mrs O'Callaghan was released but not Miss MacSwiney. This was appalling news. We knew that Miss MacSwiney was no less dangerously ill than Mrs O'Callaghan. They had been on hunger strike the same number of days, arrested in the same circumstances. It suggested malice against Miss MacSwiney that, for all we knew, might intend her death.

Our best strategic position seemed to be the top gallery, caged in with iron bars, which run round the horse-shoe shaped building and has an iron bridge joining its opposite sides. From this bridge an iron staircase runs down to the compound; it is so narrow and steep that a stretcher cannot be carried down. Miss MacSwiney's cell is on the ground floor. The prisoners marshalled themselves on the top gallery and waited. We had fastened the doors of the cells and the great well-like place was in darkness, except for one lit window beside the gateway, behind which figures of soldiers and wardresses hurried to and fro.

Our officers gave out our instructions; we were to resist, but not to attack; we were not to come to one another's rescue; no missiles were to be thrown; above all, for the patient's sake, whatever was done to us, no one must cry out. Then we knelt and said the Rosary. There was no sign of an attack. We stood three deep, arms locked, and sang, as we do every evening, some of Miss MacSwiney's favourite songs. At 10 o'clock our deputies were called to the Governor again, and after a short time they returned. Mr O'Neill, Governor of the North Dublin Union, was there; he had expressed dread of what seemed about to happen, promised that if 81 would go quietly tonight, no-one else should be removed before Miss MacSwiney was released, warned us that if we resisted, all the 'privileges' we had won through our seven-days' hunger-strike would be withdrawn; he implored us not to resist; we had ten minutes in which to decide. He was told once more that no prisoner would consent to be removed until Miss MacSwiney was released.

Ten minutes passed, then, up the staircase with a lighted taper one of the matrons came; she had seen the men who were to do the work; she was agitated and distressed; had come, on her own responsibility, to implore us to give way; they were not the military; they were CID men and military police; she could not bear the thought of their handling the girls: 'You have no idea,' she said, 'what horrible men they are.' She went down again heavy hearted; not understanding us at all. 'God pity you, girls,' she said, 'you are going into the hands of men worse than devils.'

For a little longer we waited, then, suddenly, the gate opened and the men rushed in, across the compound and up the stairs. The attack was violent but unorganised. Brigid O'Mullane and Rita Farrelly, the first seized, were crushed and bruised between men dragging them down and men pressing up the stairs.

Our Commandant, Mrs Gordon, was the next to be attacked. It was hard not to go to her rescue. She clung to the iron bars, the men beat her hands with their clenched fists again and again; that failed to make her loose her hold, and they struck her twice in the chest, then one took her head and beat it against the iron bars. I think she was unconscious after that; I saw her dragged by the soldiers down the stairs, all across the compound and out at the gate.

The men became skilled; they had many methods. Some twisted the girls' arms, some bent back their thumbs; one, who seized Iseult Stuart, kicked her on the stairs with his knee. Brigid O'Mullane, Sheila Hartnett, Roisin Ryan and Melina Phelan were kicked by a CID man who used his feet. Florence MacDermott was disabled by a blow on the ankle with a revolver; Annie McKeown, one of the smallest and youngest, was pulled downstairs and kicked, perhaps accidentally, on the head. One girl had her finger bitten. Sheila Bowen fell with a heart attack. Lily Dunn and May O'Toole, who have been very ill, fainted; they do not know where they were struck. There was one man with a blackened face. When my own turn came, after I had been dragged from the railings, a great hand closed on my face, blinding and stifling me, and thrust me back down to the ground, among trampling feet. I heard someone who saw it scream, and wondered how Miss MacSwiney would bear the noise. After that I remember being carried by two or three men and flung down in the surgery to be searched. Mrs Wilson and Mrs Gordon were there, their faces bleeding. One of the women searchers was screaming at them like a drunkard in Camden Street on Saturday night; she struck Mrs Gordon in the face. In spite of a few violent efforts to pinion us, they did not persist in searching us. They had had their lesson in Mountjoy. They contented themselves with removing watches, fountain pens and brooches, kicking Peg Flanagan and beating Kathleen O'Farrell on the head with her shoe.

I stood in the passage then, waiting for the girls to be flung out, one by one. None were frightened or overcome, but many were half fainting. Lena O'Doherty had been struck on the mouth; one man had thrust a finger down Moira Broderick's throat. Many of the men were smoking all the time – but instructions not to hit back had been well obeyed. Some soldiers who were on guard there looked wretched; the wardresses were bringing cups of water; they were crying; the prison doctor looked on smiling, smoking a cigarette, he seemed to have come for entertainment; he did nothing for the injured girl.

There was another struggle before we were thrown into the lorries, one by one, and driven away. It took five hours.

> Dorothy Macardle, Military Prison, North Dublin Union,
> 1 May 1923: *Eire*, 26 May 1923

NORTH DUBLIN UNION
The NDU had last been used as a barracks for the Black and Tans, was filthy and had no amenities. Three hundred women internees were imprisoned there, running the place themselves, on military lines.

There was plenty of open space about the rambling buildings, and here Lily McClean drilled her troops in great style. I have never seen any woman call out orders and enforce them like Captain MacClean. Drill over, the 'troops' marched round and round the compound, singing nursery rhymes, etc., to popular airs, and overlooked by the soldiers, who sat outside their hut and sometimes joined in the singing.

On our first Sunday in the North Dublin Union Mass was celebrated in the canteen. After that, an altar was set up in a large room, and we and the military knelt about anywhere. There were only a few forms for sitting on, and we seldom had a sermon; perhaps we were not sorry for that.

The weather was cold for that time of the year, and we gathered branches of trees here and there, and made a wee blaze in the huge fireplace with which the wards were fitted.

Towards the end of June the deportees were released, which left a little more breathing space in the wards. There were rumours of peace moves outside, but we were far more isolated in this camp than we were in the jails. We had little, if any, communication with the outside world, and never saw a paper.

It was about this time that I was dealt a bitter blow. A paper, some weeks old, had been found somewhere, and a group of the girls were eagerly scanning it. Presently one of them called out to me: 'What is the number of your house?' I told her. 'They've got your dump,' she called back, and read out a long list of 'stuff' which I thought was safe for ever, considering that it had escaped the search on the night of my arrest, in January, and subsequent raids. I sat down and cried ...

We had no bathing or washing facilities, and this was one of our greatest hardships. The subterfuges to which we had to have recourse to keep ourselves clean were unique. We had very little privacy: the sentries could look (and did) into the wards on the ground floor. We asked to have the lower window panes frosted or painted, but it was not done; so we had to continue to hang our clothes over them while we got into bed. No jangle of keys troubled us here; it was an open wilderness.

In our ward, on the second floor, we managed to have a bath, or rather wash, thus: a basin of water was placed in a corner of the room, and two girls held their bed blankets so as to make a curtain round the 'bather' while she performed her ablutions. This was a troublesome business, which many did not indulge in. We had difficulty too, in getting our underclothing dried; to hang it in the open was like hanging it in the street, with soldiers patrolling all over the place; to dry it in the wards would add to the dampness and mustiness of the air, so we had to improvise little lines in corridors and other places not much in use.

No wonder the thought of the North Dublin Union fills us with horror. We experienced every kind of discomfort, hunger, cold and dirt, and we were completely isolated, though only a few yards from one of the most populous districts in Dublin.

Margaret Buckley: *The Jangle of the Keys*, pp. 59-61

THE WOMEN'S PRISONERS' DEFENCE LEAGUE
One of the most effective groups to organise in support of the prisoners during the civil war was the Women's Prisoners' Defence League. The League's founder, Maud Gonne MacBride, described their work in her inimitable way.

In 1922 Cosgrave, O'Duffy and Collins took British guns and, obeying the order of Lloyd George and Winston Churchill, turned them against the republic.

Outside Mountjoy, the mothers, wives and sisters of the imprisoned republicans banded themselves together in the Women's Prisoners' Defence League.

In November of that year a thrill of horror went through Dublin at the news of the first Free State executions of young Volunteers Cassidy, Gafney, Fisher and Twohig, of Erskine Childers, and then of three more boys, Farrelly, Murphy and Spooner; on December 8, feast of the Immaculate Conception, that thrill of horror was extended to the world when General Rory O'Connor, Liam Mellows, Joe Barrett

148

and Joe McKelvey were murdered in Mountjoy Prison, without trial, by order of Cosgrave and the Executive Council.

The women of the Defence League swore that the traitors and murderers who had stained Ireland's name with such foul crimes should never be allowed to appear publicly in the city they have disgraced.

We kept our word. Our men were in jail or fighting in the country, but we women drove Cosgrave, Mulcahy and Blythe off the streets; each time they tried to hold public meetings we were there to meet them in the names of the men they had murdered. The mothers of some of the executed men were with us. Mrs Mellows, Mrs Fisher, Mrs Twohig, Mrs Gafney, Mrs Cussacks, whose son was killed in the Four Courts. Mrs Spooner's heart broke on hearing that her boy, whose letter saying he hoped to be with her for Christmas reached her the following day, was executed, and she found rest in the waters of the canal, but her old mother – Spooner's grandmother – joined the League.

The crowds were always respectful. 'Make way for the mothers of the executed, they have right to the first place,' and right up to Cosgrave's platform a way was always opened for us, us the accusers.

Where Cosgrave's secret police, the CID, had to drive us away the crowd fought round us and for us, and meeting after meeting broke up in wild confusion, till in Ireland's capital it became impossible for Cosgrave or any of his government to address the citizens, and the traitors and the murderers of Cumann na nGaedheal were reduced to carefully guarded ticket meetings in small halls.

We did this for the honour of Ireland, we did it at risk and suffering, for it is not easy for women, some of whom were old and feeble, to come out like this. Though often roughly handled and bruised, and our clothes torn, we saved Ireland's capital from the disgrace of allowing murderers and traitors to triumphantly flaunt their crimes and treason before a cowed and quiescent people. We held on till the vote of the people defeated the murderers and elected a government pledged to do justice to the dead and to the living.

> Maud Gonne MacBride: 'Must We Fight Again for Ireland's
> Honour?', *An Phoblacht*, 9 December 1933

REMEMBERING 'THE MOTHERS'

The Women's Prisoners' Dependents League was made up of the mothers of the prisoners and they were the poorest, most disadvantaged members in the movement. They were the ones with nothing, who had nothing, and that's who she worked with.

The Defence League would hold a meeting every Sunday at the corner of O'Connell Street on behalf of the prisoners and Madame MacBride would prepare her speech with the same care as if she was giving it to Congress in America, when often there would only be a rabble to hang around and listen. Mrs Despard and others would take part too, but often, often it was Madame on her own. She never missed a week.

Cumann na mBan and the Women's Prisoners' Defence League would cooperate in working for the prisoners as their work really overlapped. They would go up to the jail to find out the names of new prisoners so that they could be sent in parcels of food or clothes. Sometimes one group would send in a parcel, sometimes another.

Sighle Bean Uí Dhonnchadha (Sheila Humphreys O'Donoghue),
personal interview, 1987

CHAPTER 9

Losers in a 'Free' State

CUMANN NA mBAN RE-ORGANISES
The end of the Civil War was a time of economic hardship and despondancy for those who had been on the losing side. Cumann na mBan attempted, not too successfully, to maintain interest amongst its members.

On April 11th at 8pm a meeting of the Dublin branches of Cumann na mBan took place for the purpose of discussing a scheme of reorganisation prepared by the Re-Organising Committee of the Executive, who devised a plan whereby the organisation would continue its military training and at the same time fit itself for other spheres in the national life.

President Markievicz occupied the chair and addressed the meeting:

She advised the members to take up such special features in the reorganisation scheme as they felt they were best fitted to do. Preparations must be made for elections; social, civic and economic problems must be studied, and members should hold themselves in readiness for any eventuality which may arise: 'No one knows when we may be attacked again or when we may see our chance to strike again. Peace is beautiful and we want peace; but we cannot shirk the fight if it is the only way to win'. In her address Madam Markievicz appealed to the members to study and master the Irish language: 'They might find it difficult in the beginning but most things that are worth doing are not easy'. The subject of unemployment, its causes and suggestions for assisting its alleviation brought the presidential address to a close.

The Director of Training read a scheme of organisation:

Lectures
Given fortnightly by well-known speakers, including historical, social and economic subjects. Lecturers will be asked to recommend books on the subject of the lecture, to be read by members. In connection with this, the Executive will endeavour to procure books which will form the nucleus of a library. Lectures in the Irish language will be given periodically.

Choir

Under the supervision of a qualified choral mistress, to be formed immediately and to be open to all members desirous of joining.

First Aid

A special class, conducted by an expert instructor, will be formed. Regular attendance to be compulsory for this branch of work. On termination of the course an examination will be held and certificates awarded.

Branch Meetings

To be held monthly, at which military and physical drill will be given ... if these meetings are well attended, and it is thought advisable, the number of meetings per month will be increased. In connection wtih 'jerks' class, drill displays will be arranged.

Officers' Class

In order that branches be drilled efficiently, an Officers' Training Class will be started as soon as all branch elections have taken place.

Games – Camogie and Rounders

Teams will be formed in branches where possible, and inter-branch matches will be fixed by a Games Committee, which will be elected by the players from all branches ... In this way members from all over the country will get to know each other and a spirit of self-reliance, comradeship and discipline will be fostered.

The foregoing scheme will be started in Dublin and as far as possible, spread to the country branches. In order to keep the country in touch with what is going on in Dublin and to assist branches in the country to reorganise, Cumann na mBan notes and activities will be inserted in 'Eire' from time to time.

The scheme was enthusiastically approved.

Eire, 31 May 1924

CUMANN NA mBAN AND THE ANTI-JUROR CAMPAIGN

To Irish Citizens –
'Break the Connection with the British Empire'

The enemies of Ireland are imprisoning the men and women who are carrying out the only practical programme to attain freedom.

Unfortunately some of Dublin's degenerate and slavish citizens assist them in this work. Last month the following: (12 names and addresses) – helped Corrigan and the infamous 'Judge' Sullivan to send the Irish patriot CON HEALY to penal servitude for 5 years. These men are traitors to their country.

(Death would be their fate in any free country in the world.)

Issued by *'Ghosts'*, n.d. (1929). National Library of Ireland

'THE MOTHERS' RESISTANCE

The bitterness engendered by the Civil War and the continued determination of the Free State government to crush the republican dissidents led to the imposition of increasingly coercive measures. The women's organisation 'The Mothers' maintained their opposition.

With the coming of Mr Cosgrave's Coercion Act last October the Women's Prisoner's Defence League found itself starred among the twelve banned organisations. Immediately it became a question how we were to defeat the ban and carry on our publicity at the same time. From 1922, every week, our meetings had been held uninterruptedly in 'the ruins' of O'Connell St. We shifted from one ruined site to another as re-building began. We watched O'Connell St. rise again from its ashes and finally made our pitch in Cathal Brugha St., which we helped to name. For our League had survived all the other Coercion Acts of the Cosgrave regime, neither police nor military ever succeeding in removing 'The Mothers' (as the League was popularly called) from the streets or from the jail gates, though Free State Military had once turned a machine gun on one of our meetings, killing a woman, and though they and the CID. fired at us on several occasions.

So now we bought and studied a copy of Mr Cosgrave's 'Seventeenth Amendment to the Constitution Act', realising that the most important work before the WPDL was to give publicity to its amazing provisions. Few people had even read the Coercion Act. We felt that if we could focus public attention on the sections of that Act which forbade coroners' inquests upon the deaths of prisoners, which empowered any policeman or soldier holding the rank of Officer, to arrest without warrant and charge any persons (even young girls), and to take them to any place at their discretion and to search and detain them for days, it would bring down the Cosgrave Government in ignominy. All meetings of banned organisations were forbidden and the press muzzled.

We were evicted from our Office in Middle Abbey Street, shared with another of the banned organisations. The office not being in our name, we could not resist and found it impossible to get an office anywhere, for under the Act every house harbouring a banned organisation would be closed by the police. So the Committee of the League arranged for weekly teas at Woolworth's. These soon became famous. Pressmen came to interview us at them; soon the CID started taking tea at neighbouring tables. Arriving late one day, a newsboy outside told me 'all your friends are waiting for you upstairs.' So we had to vary days, hours and cafes. Bewley's café was as convenient as Woolworth's: so we went there next. Sometimes the more public the meeting place the greater the protection afforded.

The first Sunday after the Coercion Act became law immense crowds waited in O'Connell Street to see if the usual weekly meeting could be held. Squads of uniformed police and CID stood round. At the usual time our lorry-platform drove up bearing a large canvas scroll with 'People's Rights Association'. The driver, questioned by the police, said that he had been paid by a lady who said she was the secretary of the People's Rights Association. A police superintendent consulted the long list of banned organisations. The People's Rights Association was not on the list! CID men at his elbow urged him to stop the meeting, but he shook his head; he had no power to prevent any but the banned organisations holding public meetings. A smile crossed his face when Mrs Despard and a number of speakers got on the platform. As chairwoman I announced that, at a time when the liberties of the people were being taken from them, the People's Rights Association had come into being to defend those liberties and, book in hand, we were going to expound on Mr Cosgrave's 17th Amendment of the Constitution. The superintendent's smile grew anxious when Miss Moloney, quoting Shakespeare, said, amid tremendous applause from the crowd, 'A Rose by any other name would smell as sweet!' The Mothers had won the first round and went home contented.

Maud Gonne MacBride: 'How We Beat the Terrorist Proclamations', *An Phoblacht*, 12 November 1932

WOMEN'S PART IN THE REVOLUTIONARY STRUGGLE

Nora Connolly O'Brien, daughter of James Connolly, analysed the role played by women during the various stages of the struggle against Britain. Her conclusion was that women in the Ireland of the 1930s were in danger of losing all the gains they had made.

In the Proclamation of the Republic in 1916 the leaders of the Republican movement declared that Irishmen and women were citizens sharing equal rights and opportunities, and claimed the allegiance of both.

We are proud to think that our nation was the first to proclaim the equal rights of men and women; and sometimes dimly and vaguely remember that the distinction between the sexes and subjection of one to the other was a foreign institution foisted upon us, among many other iniquities, by an alien Government. And, curiously enough, we women whisper in our hearts now and again, the only one completely accepted and cherished by the men of our nation. Only the deep sense of justice, instinctive in women, has prevented us from holding them wholly inexcusable.

For centuries we seemed content to be 'the slaves of that slave' and, in the words of James Connolly, exhibited in our martyrdom 'a most damnable patience.' In that we are to blame, 'duties' we accepted, 'rights' we never claimed, and thus induced in the minds of our menfolk, of each succeeding generation, a placid acceptance of our inferior status in the nation.

James Connolly was always an apostle for women's rights and equality. Time and time again he proclaimed that no movement was assured of success that had not women in it. 'Win the women to your cause and your cause is secure,' he said. He pointed out that the fact that women have 'ever proven valuable assets in every progressive movement in Ireland is evidence of the great value their co-operation will be when, to their self-sacrificing acceptance of duty they begin to unite its necessary counterpoise, a high-minded assertion of rights.'

In all his activities he sought their co-operation, strove to make them articulate and insistent on their rights, to realise their power and to wield it. He resented the training which for centuries had caused Irish womanhood to surrender its rights and claimed that as a consequence of that surrender 'the race had lost its chief capacity to withstand assaults from without and demoralisation from within,' and which consciously or unconsciously was fashioning a slave mentality.

To him, women in a movement must not, as a matter of course, be the drudges of that movement, performing its arduous, inglorious, and thankless tasks, meekly submitting themselves to the domination of the men, and denying themselves a voice in its policy. That, he held, would be disastrous to the movement; would be a conscious deliberate aid to the continued demoralisation and degradation of the race to which no truly patriotic Irishman could give countenance.

It is interesting to note in this connection that the only woman sentenced to death in 1916 and the one woman wounded on active service and bearing arms in 1916, were members of the Irish Citizen Army of which he was the dominant figure. The more active part women took in a movement the greater his pleasure; by his advice and counsel he encouraged them; more, he gave them often that little extra push forward they needed. He saw nothing incongruous in a woman having a seat on an army council, or preferring to bear arms to winding bandages.

Perhaps he saw in that preference a resurgence of the ancient Irish instinct dormant since the days when the Brehon Laws held sway. In ancient Ireland land, at first, was only divided amongst the male members of the family. This was changed through the activities of the wife of a Brehon, who had studied the laws to such advantage that her representations won for women not only possession of land but equality in general. Her main argument was that women were equally free with the clansmen and *like them were liable to bear arms in the muster of the clan.*

The women of Ireland of every generation have both actively and passively aided the struggle for freedom since the coming of the British. In the main, that has been unwritten history, only the romantic side of the picture has been painted. But some day some writer will choose the humble life of Anne Devlin, who was whipped at the cart and half-hanged several times, yet refused to betray the hiding place of Robert Emmet, or, will tell of Betsy Gray who fought and died on the battlefield in '98; or, of Mary Ann McCracken in Belfast and the many arduous tasks, and the risks to life and liberty which she undertook on behalf of the United Irishmen; or, of the heroines of 1916 and 1918-21 and 1922-23. Here is romantic history greater than any love story ever written – the love of a woman for her country, her cheerful disregard of danger, her lack of consideration for health, liberty, or life. There is no townland that has not its tale to tell, nor a city that has not a hundred tales of girls dropping their everyday task and setting on a deed of high endeavour, recking nothing of its dangers, accomplishing it, and calmly returning once more to their everyday tasks.

It is regrettable that Irishwomen should have that ability to return to the everyday task that having won the right to share in the dangers of war, they should have relinquished their right to share in the dangers of peace.

Progressive and revolutionary women have no voice in the council of the revolutionary movement. Revolutionary women are today showing once more that 'damnable patience' and are content to be the drudges of the movement. The men and women of the revolutionary movement would do well to take heed of the warning of James Connolly that a continuance of this policy will cause the race to lose 'its capacity to withstand the assaults from without and the demoralisation from within.'

The past few years have given evidence that we have not been able to withstand the assaults from without nor the demoralisation from within and it behoves us to take time and thought to discover the reason. And if, as some of us think, the salvation of the country is to be found in the doctrines of James Connolly then, we must not exclude his doctrine on the place of women in Ireland.

The revolutionary men and women must insist that men and women in Ireland have equal rights and duties and a surrender of any one of those rights or duties is treason to Ireland.

> Nora Connolly O'Brien: 'Women in Ireland, Their Part in the Revolutionary Struggle', *An Phoblacht*, 25 June 1932

CUMANN NA mBAN CONVENTION 1933

The Cumann na mBan Convention of 1933 witnessed a significant change in policy. Rather than cling to the fantasy that the 'Second Dáil' of 1921 was still the legitimate government, the organisation took the decision to pledge allegiance to the ideals expressed in the 1916 Proclamation of the Republic. In protest, Mary MacSwiney and Caitlin and Nodlaig Brugha resigned their membership.

Delegates from every part of Ireland attended a general Convention of Cumann na mBan, which was held in Dublin, on Saturday and Sunday, 10th and 11th June.

The Convention was presided over by Eithne Ni Chumhaill, President, who in the course of her address reviewed the Republican situation since the first Convention of Cumann na mBan nineteen years ago – the many parting of the ways which had come since then, when Cumann na mBan had taken the lead in showing the people of Ireland the real road to Freedom. The object for which the Organisation was founded was still unachieved and the work before the Cumann na mBan was to end that infamous Treaty of 1921 and set up a Free Ireland according to the Proclamation of Easter Week, 1916, where there will be equal rights and equal opportunities for all its citizens, an Ireland where the poor shall cease to be exploited for the benefit of the rich, an Ireland that will be a shining light that the nations of the earth shall envy, and not the miserable partitioned colony in which we are unfortunately compelled to live today.

She referred to Partition – one of the greatest tragedies of our history – which was becoming more and more glaring every day. The shameful display each Easter around the Cemeteries inside this artificial barrier by order of Sir Dawson Bates was a disgrace to our race and a state of affairs which should not be tolerated. This question of Partition should be faced seriously, we should endeavour by every means in our power to smash this tyranny, we must show those tyrants in the North that the land of Ulster belongs to the real people of Ireland and not to the planter stock of Henry VIII. She emphasised the need for extending the Organisation to every part of Ireland, in order that its members may be able to spread the Separatist Doctrine and convince the people of Ireland that in that Doctrine lay our National salvation.

The Secretary's report gave a detailed account of the Organisation's activities during the last 18 months. The Organisation was stronger throughout the country than it had been for many years. Many new Branches had come into existence and prospects for the future were full of promise.

Publicity, through distribution of literature had been done on a very large scale, particularly during the time of the Eucharistic Congress when an Information Bureau was set up at Headquarters where visitors of all Nationalities called.

The Easter Lily campaign, which had been initiated by Cumann na mBan in 1926 was increasing in popularity each succeeding year, as was shown by the satisfactory report from the treasurer.

Cumann na gCailiní: an organisation for girls between the ages of 8 and 16 had been founded by the Executive and had now spread to many centres. The object of this Organisation is to foster in the minds of the girls of Ireland a desire for freedom of their country and the welfare of its people, by making Irish their everyday language; educating them in the History of their country, and training them in all the qualities needed to fit them to take their place in a free and Gaelic Ireland.

Belfast Prisoners: Last October, when the workers of Belfast made such a splendid stand against Imperialism, the Executive organised a Flag Day for the victims of the fight, which met with a most generous response from all parts of the country. Two members of the Belfast Branch – Mary Donnelly and Sarah Grimley – served sentences of 2 and 3 months in Armagh Jail for their activities in connection with the visit of the Prince of Wales to Belfast last year.

Treasurer's Report: Showed the Finances of the Organisation to be in a very sound position.

Constitutional Changes: From their experience in organising throughout the country, the Executive had come to the conclusion that a slight alteration in the Constitution was necessary. Hitherto Article 1 of the Constitution read: 'Cumann na mBan is an independent body of Irishwomen, pledged to maintain the Irish Republic established on January 21st, 1919, and to organise and train the women of Ireland to work unceasingly for its international recognition. All women of Irish birth or descent are eligible for membership, except that no woman who is a member of the enemy organisation, or who does not recognise the Government of the Republic as the lawfully constituted

Government of the people can become a member.' It has been altered to read: 'Cumann na mBan is an independent body of Irishwomen pledged to maintain the Irish Republic proclaimed in Easter Week 1916, and to organise and train the women of Ireland to put into effect the ideals and obligations contained in that Proclamation. All women of Irish birth or descent are eligible for membership, except those who are members of an enemy organisation. Members must never render allegiance to any government but a Republican government for all Ireland.'

The reason which prompted the Executive to make this alteration was that it had become evident that to confine membership of the Organisation to those who believed in the existence of the Second Dáil was to isolate ourselves from the growing generation and to make progress towards our goal impossible. It was felt that the fundamental principle of an Organisation should be based on a belief to which members can freely subscribe and while, to many women who have lived through the setting up of Dáil Eireann, its existence is a matter of deep significance, to ask young girls and women to render allegiance to a Government which does not and cannot function is simply taxing their powers of credulity beyond reasonable bounds.

On a vote the alteration was adopted with only 7 dissenters.

On the results being announced, Miss Mary MacSwiney and two other delegates said they were forced with deep regret to intimate their intention to resign. Despite a unanimous appeal from the whole Organisation to remain members, the three delegates could not be induced to alter their decision.

Important Resolutions:

Social Policy: Since the aim is in accordance with the Proclamation, it was decided to embark on a campaign to propagate social reconstruction on lines laid down by James Connolly.

Partition: an intensive campaign in the north of Ireland setting forth the ideals of a Christian State organised on the National and Social Principles of the Proclamation.

Boycott British: to organise an intensive campaign throughout the year.

Cinemas: to get managers to show special films for children.

Eithne Ni Chumhaill was unanimously re-elected as President, together with an Executive representative of Dublin.

An Phoblacht, 24 June 1933; *Irish Freedom*, June 1933

MNÁ NA POBLACHTA
(WOMEN OF THE REPUBLIC)

Mná na Poblachta is the only women's organisation that stands for the maintenance and defence of the living Republic of Ireland, proclaimed in arms, Easter 1916, established by the free will of the Irish people, 21st January 1919 and never since disestablished.

Mná na Poblachta has been formed by members of Cumann na mBan who resigned from that organisation as a result of its decision at the historic Convention of June 1933 to abandon Dáil Eireann, the Government of the Republic, and thus violating the fundamental principle of its Constitution.

Mná na Poblachta aims at organising and training the women and girls of Ireland for the purpose of breaking the connection with England, helping the Government of the Republic in the exercise of its functions as the lawfully constituted Government of All-Ireland, and securing for the Republic international recognition.

Mná na Poblachta maintains and defends the Irish Republic against its enemies, foreign and domestic.

Mná na Poblachta denies the authority and opposes the will of enemy institutions.

Mná na Poblachta trains its members to help and sustain soldiers and citizens in the maintenance and defence of the Republic.

Mná na Poblachta fosters an Irish atmosphere, nationally, socially and economically.

Mná na Poblachta is open for membership to all women of Irish birth or descent who accept the Constitution and Rules on this, the 11th Anniversary of the murder of the Four Martyrs, appeals to the women and girls of Ireland to enrol in its ranks and help to complete the task undertaken in every generation by the manhood and womanhood of Ireland – for a free and independent Irish nation.

The Hon. Sec., Nodlaig Brugha, 8 December 1933:
Mná na Poblachta, leaflet. National Library of Ireland

'THE GREAT IDEAL OF CUMANN NA mBAN'

As part of the drive to educate its membership, a series of lectures given by the executive of Cumann na mBan were published in An Phoblacht. *The themes combined the social and economic philosophy of James Connolly with the economic protectionism of the early Sinn Féin movement. Overall, the content displayed an unsophisticated ideal which largely reflected the rural backgrounds of most of the membership.*

In the Ireland we in Cumann na mBan are working for, every child would have the freedom to choose whatever livelihood he wishes, freedom to avail of the best schools, and the best universities.

British rule in Ireland has meant oppression, ignorance, almost extermination of our language and the culture it represents, for the vast majority of the people. Freedom must mean the restoration of power, education, opportunities and their language to all the people of Ireland.

Should freedom not mean the restoration of these equal rights and opportunities, far better that we remain in BRITISH slavery.

In the Ireland we in Cumann na mBan are working for, there would be no such thing as hunger. A 'free' Ireland in which even one man or woman suffered hunger would disgrace the name of freedom. In a free Ireland the land would be used not to fatten bullocks for John Bull, but to grow food for all.

British rule has meant the turning of our arable land into pasture land. British rule ensured our depending on England for our dáily bread. If Freedom means anything it surely means freedom to feed our people. Freedom without the power to feed the people is a mockery of the word. In the Ireland we in Cumann na mBan are working for no excuse of private property or vested interest would be permitted to keep food from the people.

In the Ireland we of Cumann na mBan are working for, every man and woman and child would be clothed in Irish made clothes. We were famous all over Europe for our woollen tweeds; this industry would be revived, and its production and distribution would be organised by the Government with a view to the needs of the people.

Flax would be grown for the making of linen to provide the necessary requirements for home consumption and later for export.

Special attention would be devoted to the providing of boots for the whole nation.

In the Ireland we of Cumann na mBan are working for, the natural resources of the country in mines, bogs, etc., would be used to provide fuel for all the people, and not as at present to make money for the owners of the bogs and mines.

In the free Ireland we of Cumann na mBan are working for, there must be no slums, no tenement houses. Dwellers in slums and tenements do not know what freedom is.

As women, we in Cumann na mBan have a special interest and obligation to see that proper houses are provided for every family in the country. In the Ireland we are working for there will not be different classes of houses for different classes of people. Freedom must mean the best houses that brains can plan and hands can build for every family in the country.

As prevention is better than cure, every effort shall be made to maintain the highest standard of health among all the people in the country. Every assistance will be given to the advance of medical science. All forms of medical service shall be free for all.

To sum up, it may be said that we in Cumann na mBan are working for an Ireland in which not a few fortunate individuals – but ALL shall enjoy the maximum amount of happiness which God permits in this passage of suffering and sorrow.

And now that you know what you mean by freedom and an Irish Republic you should avail of every opportunity to explain your aims and objects as it is chiefly through ignorance and a complete failure to understand our aims that the people fail to support us as they should, and secure the support of all the people in our struggle.

An Phoblacht, 7 October 1933

CONDITIONS OF EMPLOYMENT BILL

In 1935 the government introduced the Conditions of Employment Bill, some clauses of which were intended to ensure that the limited number of jobs in the industrial sector went to men rather than to women. Cumann na mBan did not become involved in protests against the Bill; however, amongst the figures involved in the protests were women who had been active in the nationalist movement for many years.

The Irish Women Workers Union held a protest meeting at the Mansion House on November 20. It was presided over by Miss C. Fagan. Louie Bennett, secretary of the Irish Women Workers' Union, moved the resolution:

'Deploring the growing tendency in the country to evade democratic principles and to give unrestricted powers to Government Ministers, and protesting against any infringement of the principle of equality of rights granted under the Constitution, and in particular against that section of the Conditions of Employment Bill which proposed arbitrary limitation of employment for women.'

The Minister for Industry and Commerce (she declared) is building up the framework of an industrial state which will hold under the control of his Department, all the industries of the country. Under the Control of Manufactures Act he had a grip upon manufacturers, and he could and did tighten that grip by subsidies, concessions and promises of monopolies.

By this Bill, women's security of employment was placed unreservedly in the power of the Minister for Industry. They had no power to appeal against any arbitrary decision he might make, and it must be clearly understood that his motive was not concern for the welfare of women workers.

Dorothy Macardle seconded the resolution. She said that their campaign was only part of a necessary world-wide campaign for women's independence. The Bill only asked that a person should be male in order that he should get employment; the questions of dependence or responsibility were not mentioned.

Mr A. Wood KC said it was a Bill which would neither benefit men nor women workers, and they should not only protest against it, but rebel against it. 'It is a dastardly attempt on the part of a reactionary Government', he said 'to turn back the hands on the face of progress.'

Dr Ethna Byrne MA, Assistant Lecturer in English, UCD, said that women were no longer in practice obtaining higher Civil Service posts; there was a great depression in the secondary school teaching profession, and women primary teachers were now compelled to retire on marriage.

Professor Mary Hayden, representing the National Council of Women in Ireland, moved:

'That this meeting, realising the tragedy of unemployment for men or women, declares its conviction that to impose its miseries upon women in order to provide work for men is a method which would only serve to deepen poverty and create new types of unemployment, and, therefore, as an alternative, urges the Government to provide more work for men by initiating public works of national utility.'

In no country had so sweeping a measure to the detriment of women been attempted or passed as that Bill which they were now considering.

Mrs Hanna Sheehy-Skeffington MA, seconding, said that Mr Lemass's attitude was that of a Fascist dictator. There was much talk about religion at present, but it was immoral to let young women be driven out of jobs perhaps when they had old and infirm dependents. There was a terrible alternative such unfortunate women might take, and it would be at the door of Mr Lemass and other politicans if women were driven to take that alternative.

Men who would displace women under such circumstances were nothing short of blacklegs. Women should go further now and point out to Mr Lemass that many of his so-called factories were really sweat-shops.

Professor R.W. Dichburn said that the effects of the Bill on male employment would only be a drop in the ocean. Unemployment among men to be seriously tackled required much greater schemes of public money.

Mrs Buckley said that, generally speaking, women were driven into industry by economic pressure.

Miss H. Moloney said that the Trades Union Congress had fought with all its power against the Bill and against that clause affecting women. The Labour Party had also made representation to get the clause deleted, but although Mr Lemass received the deputation with politeness, he treated the application with contempt.

The resolution was passed.

Republican Congress, 30 November 1935

THE 1937 CONSTITUTION

With the introduction of the 1937 Constitution, the defeat of women's hopes for an equality of status in the twenty-six county state was complete. Prison Bars, *edited by Maud Gonne MacBride as a small news-sheet for the Women's Prisoners' Dependents League, was now the only paper edited by a woman. It published objections to the Constitution from women who had been prominent within the nationalist movement.*

Hanna Sheehy-Skeffington

We have had already two Constitutions. In the first, which could fit on a fair-sized sheet of notepaper, citizenship for women and equal rights and equal opportunities were guaranteed. Had the Irish Republic been set up then, Irish women would have had votes years before their British sisters, who got partial suffrage only in 1918. As it was, Constance Markievicz was the only woman elected in 1918 for the British House of Commons and she later held the post of Cabinet Minister for Labour under Dáil Eireann.

Following the acceptance of the Treaty by a majority of seven, a new Constitution was published on the day of the election (1922). As far as women were concerned, it carried out, if more formally and not quite so wholeheartedly, the intention of the 1916 Proclamation.

Mr de Valera's Constitution runs:
40. All citizens shall, as human persons, be held equal before the law. This shall not mean that the State shall not in its enactments have due regard to differences of capacity, physical and moral and of social functions.
41. (2) 1. In particular the State recognises that by her life within the home woman gives to the State a support without which the common good cannot be achieved.

2. The State shall therefore endeavour to ensure that mothers shall not be obliged by economic necessity to engage in labour to the neglect of their duties at home.

45. 4. Sub-section 2. The State shall endeavour to ensure that the inadequate strength of women shall not be abused and that women or children shall not be forced to enter avocations unsuited to their sex, age or strength.

There is no woman in Mr de Valera's Cabinet and but two in his Party. No woman appears to have been consulted by him. He and his Party are up against the entire body of organised women. From all sides, from the Women Workers Union (consisting of women trade unionists) to the Women Graduates at both Universities, the Joint Societies of various Women's organisations, the National Council of Women, a clamour of protest has arisen. Many supporters of Mr de Valera have bombarded him and his party. The Opposition (whose record towards women is in the main no better, but oppositions are politicans and naturally exploit their opportunities) has taken up the matter.

Never before have women been so united as now when they are faced with Fascist proposals endangering their livelihood, cutting away their rights as human beings. The outcome will probably be the formation of a Woman's Party; meanwhile a special emergency committee has been set up and a fighting fund inaugurated.

Mr de Valera is thoroughly angry and full of declarations that his words do not mean what they seem. He says he only means to honour mothers in the home and that there is now no need to emphasise equality, as we have it! When pressed upon the 'inadequate strength' reference he says it means women should not be miners or navvies.

Mr de Valera shows mawkish distrust of women which has always coloured his outlook; his was the only command in Easter Week where the help of women (of the Cumann na mBan, women's auxiliary to the Irish Volunteers) was refused. He sent the women home; some went to other areas and were welcomed, and de Valera, as I heard him say somewhat sheepishly years later, 'lost some good men who had to be cooks in their place' ... Connolly, in his Citizen Army, would have welcomed women as soldiers were they so minded, and he saw to it long before that those that were, had military training ...

De Valera has refused to alter, except that he has restored 'without distinction of sex' for voting purposes. He has refused to restore 1916 Equal Rights and Equal Opportunities for Women.

Kathleen Clarke

Mrs Clarke, ex-TD, ex-Senator, widow of Tom Clarke, first Signatory of the Proclamation of the Republic; in a letter read at the great

Protest Meeting of Women called in the Mansion House, Dublin, by the Women Graduates Association, stated:

'The rights accorded in the Proclamation were the result of the considered opinion, after lengthy deliberation, of the minds of seven men who, I have heard President de Valera say, were supermen. They were not intended as a mere gesture to be set aside when (or if) success crowned the fight for freedom.

The langauge is simple, unequivocal, and can be interpreted only one way, whereas the language of the proposed Constitution may be interpreted in more ways than one.

Therefore, I think it is up to every Irishwomen to see that no man or group of men, robs us of our status enshrined in that Proclamation.'

Kate O'Callaghan

Mrs O'Callaghan, widow of Michael O'Callaghan, Mayor of Limerick, and woman TD in Republican Dáil, writing from St. Margaret's, Tivoli, Limerick, said:

'My main objection to the Constitution is based on its acceptance of the British Crown and membership of the British Group of Nations, an acceptance veiled by the untrue declaration in Article 5, that 'Eire is a sovereign, independent, and democratic State.' This fundamental objection is strengthened by other features in the document, none more than by the articles dealing with women. These articles I regard as a betrayal of the 1916 promise of 'Equal Rights and Equal Opportunities guaranteed to all citizens.' They are a grave danger to the future position of women and I hope that the National University Women Graduates Association will do good work in putting this danger before the eyes of the intelligent women of the community.'

Maud Gonne MacBride

Prevented by illness from attending the meeting on Monday, Madame Gonne MacBride wrote:

'With one of our provinces cut off, and the Republican Army outlawed and 44 Republicans in jail and hundreds of good men in their keeping, it seems absurd to talk of a permanent Constitution for Ireland. We have the Proclamation of the Republic a noble, clear, concise Document, as our Charter of Liberty. It has been endorsed by the whole nation. The substitution of another Document is a weakening of our national position.

If, when Ireland is free, a more detailed Constitution were needed the Article concerning women, and the Articles providing for Special Courts in Mr de Valera's Draft Constitution would damn it in my eyes.'

Prison Bars, July 1937

THE WOMEN'S SOCIAL AND PROGRESSIVE LEAGUE

The Women's Social and Progressive League asks you to consider carefully the following facts and to reassure youself before casting your vote for any candidate as to his or her attitude on matters vitally concerning the position of women. Do not accept platitudes. Under the Constitution our position has deteriorated and is further menaced by the implications of Clauses 40, 41 and 45.

Women Workers – Already in the Tailoring Trade women are being dispensed with in favour of men and boys!

Women Teachers (Primary) – Women teachers (no longer employed as they are in other countries after marriage) are now being compulsorily retired at 60, thus deprived of their full pension rights which can only be gained by 40 years service. Both these victimisations of women have taken place since the passage of the Constitution.

Women Teachers (Secondary) – The incremental salary paid by the government to women is on a lower scale and reaches a lower maximum than that paid to men.

Women Agricultural Workers – Women and girls who work in the field, yard or farm, have no fixed rates of wages, though there is a fixed rate of pay for the male worker.

Civil Service Discriminates Against Women – In the Civil Service women have neither the same pay nor the same opportunities of promotion as men. The State, which should be an exemplary employer, discriminates against women, and thus sets an evil example to all other employees of labour in the country. Women are the lowest paid in the Civil Service and are being used to scale-down the grading and pay of all civil servants. All this discrimination against women is causing increased emigration of women and girls, to countries where better opportunities are available.

Professional Women – In all professional posts under the Government, a much inferior salary and inferior conditions are offered to women – a glaring injustice and in marked contrast to their treatment by the local authorities and by the universities.

Jury Service – Women are barred from Jury Service, which means that women are deprived of the right of being tried by their peers. Increasingly, women are ignored by the big political parties, even under Proportional Representation. If PR is abolished, the restoration of the single-member constituency would not only affect all minority groups, but militate further against the selection of any women candidates.

Instances could be multiplied of discrimination against women in practically every walk of life. This menace can only be met by women taking active measures to resist such encroachments upon their rights as citizens.

DO NOT VOTE for any candidate, however plausible pre-election promises may be, unless you are satisfied that he or she will defend your interests and guarantee your equal right of citizenship.

> Women voters wake up!
> Join the W.S.P.L.

> Women's Social and Progressive League: *Open Letter to Women Voters of Ireland*, 1938, leaflet. National Library of Ireland

A LAST FIGHT – THE CHALLENGE OF WOMEN INDEPENDENTS

In the 1943 elections four women stood on an independent, pro-woman platform – the forerunner, it was hoped, of a woman's party. All lost. Hanna Sheehy-Skeffington, one of the candidates, wrote an article in which she reflected on the spirit of the times.

Is the Dáil a fit place for Women? The answer of the electorate would appear to be No. THE BELL in a recent issue expressed strongly the view that more women – independent of party – are badly needed to play their part in national housekeeping; other organs of opinion, including DUBLIN OPINION, expressed the same view, backed by many individuals of various (and of no) party politics; so did several women's societies, led by the Women's Social and Progressive League, which launched a campaign.

Four women stood at the recent General Election as independents, pledged to a programme mainly, though not exclusively, addressed to women-voters, standing for freedom from party affiliations. Their platform stressed the need for greater representation of women in the councils of the nation and their slogans included 'Equal Pay for Equal Work', 'Equal Opportunities for Women', the removal of the many disabilities economic, social and domestic that still restrict women; their election literature stated – ' there can be no true democracy when the voice of half the community is silent in Parliament.' That women should be elected to play their part in 'Leinster Housekeeping' was their plea as housewives to whom education, the care of the young, the old, the sick, are largely entrusted. Two women, Miss Corbett and Miss Phillips, stood in Tipperary (one of our largest counties, with two Ridings and two Councils, yet forming only one constituency). Both were active members of the Irish Country Women's Association, with experience on local bodies: they conducted a joint lightening campaign over their big area. Miss Margaret Ashe stood for Galway, where she has for several years been Chairman of the Council and is an able administratrix. The writer of this article stood for South Dublin, choosing that area because she represented it for two terms of office in the then Sinn Féin party (which had 5 women councillors between 1918 and 1925). Thus for the first time in both city and country districts Independent women stood for the Dáil: a notable nucleus of a Women's Party. (In Great Britain there are now 14 women MPs. With one exception, Miss Rathbone, who represents the Universities and is an Independent, all belong to parties and are selected and run by the party machine – not, of course, under PR, but under the single-member scheme which should make the selection of a woman much harder. They are, one Liberal, four Labour and eight Conservatives; one from Wales, two from Scotland, and the rest from English constituencies. All are trained women who are especially articulate and effective on questions affecting women.)

Our experiment, a bold enough challenge to masculine monopoly, failed. We were all beaten. Only one, Miss Ashe, retained her £100 deposit. The various parties, all but Fianna Fail, which is the most conservative where women are concerned, put up new candidates. Labour put up one, Miss Crowley, in Cork; Fine Gael one in Dublin County, Miss Ennis; and the Farmer's Party Miss Bobbett, the organiser of the Party. In this constituency the two women divided votes, unfortunately, while in Cork the woman had no chance as the constituency could not carry even the sitting TD. Parties have a way of running two women in the same constituency in the hope of dividing votes, in others of running a woman as an 'extra' where she has not an earthly hope of winning.

The net result therefore was that the same three women previously elected – Mrs Rice, Mrs Redmond, and Mrs Reynolds, called often 'the three Rs', also 'the Silent Sisters,' were returned. All are widows of former TDs. The first is Fianna Fail, the other two Fine Gael. They are obedient party women and have never shown any interest in questions affecting women. Thus, in a total of 138, the eleventh Dáil has still but three women TDs. The first had six, one a Cabinet Minister, Countess Markievicz, Minister for Labour in the Republican Dáil; the first woman elected in 1918 to the House of Commons at the first election after women received the vote – it was limited then to women over 30. (No British woman was then returned, and, ironically, the only woman MP, then under a life-sentence in Holloway Jail, did not sit. Ireland led then as to feminine representation: now it has fallen back. It is also interesting to note that all the Republican women deputies voted against the Treaty: since then there appears to be a slump, after the other side won out.)

There are certain areas – though our country has a majority of males – where there are more women-voters on the register than men. This year, furthermore, a large number of men-voters, particularly in the cities, were absent in Britain, no means being afforded them to register their vote legitimately: though there is little doubt that many 'voted' nevertheless. The following facts refer to the constituency, Dublin South City, in which I stood. There are seven seats and over 82,000 names are on the register. Of these 42,000 are women. As the Government sprang the election, giving only the briefest possible notice – many experts believed up to the last moment, for the secret was well kept, that there would be no General Election – all organisations, save Fianna Fail, had a difficult task, the Women Independents an almost insuperable one. In Dublin our venue was chosen in South City partly because of my previous connection therewith municipally, partly because its seven seats seemed to afford a better chance for an Independent, and partly because Mr Lemass, Minister for Supplies, was standing, whose ministry was under fire for many reasons owing to potato shortage, bread queues, coupon crises and the like. South Dublin is mainly a working-class area, and the voters could, if agreed, have returned the majority of the seven TDs. Voting was over 60 per cent of those on the register: the voters had 19 candidates on the panel to choose from, representing a wide choice, Fianna Fail, Fine Gael, Labour, Coras na Poblachta (a new group) and independents – of whom the man, Mr Rice, was the typical Business-Conservative.

I built up my platform on James Connolly's Republic, which included feminism, for Connolly did not restrict freedom to one sex. He said (I quoted it in my election address): – 'The woman worker is the slave of a slave.' South City seemed for all these reasons favourable ground.

Under PR if voters cast their votes in order of personal preference rather than party – they do not, as it happens – there should have been enough First Preferences for the woman to stay the course until she got sufficient second votes from eliminations to be returned. This did not happen, however, though eleven of the men walked the plank, eight losing deposits. Mr Lemass topped the poll with the big figure (larger than his chief's, Mr de Valera's) of 16,000 first preferences, and surplus enough to carry in three more of his party with him. Fine Gael had enough of the Big Business element in the area to secure two seats, and Labour (in this predominantly Labour area) got just one seat. Ironically this Minister, who has often boldly declared himself an opponent of woman suffrage, holding that women are sufficiently 'represented' by their nearest male relative, owes his return apparently to the votes of women.

So what? Will women not vote for women? They did that in the first Dáil and still do in municipal elections. Do voters dislike

Independents? Possibly. Were the dice loaded in favour of Fianna Fail? All these factors counted. Women, the average and sub-average, still have that inferiority complex, just as there were negro-slaves who were opposed to emancipation. Yet they did vote for women in the areas where the three previously-elected women TDs stood. The party machine (true this of all the parties) is still male and still allergic to women, most of all, naturally, to Independents. (The Independent man too is disliked, because he is not amenable to the party whip.) Other factors are the increased cost of elections. Where £300 would formerly be enough running expenses £1,000 would now be needed. Shortness of time was another handicap, for many experts declined to the last to believe that any election would take place: when it did, an appeal was successfully made to Panic – the 'Don't-swap-horses-crossing-a-stream' and 'Dev-will-keep-you-out-of-the-war' arguments. The women suffered a press boycott, that paper wall Griffith used to talk of as round Ireland, wrapped them round: and though posters did speak, they were not enough.

Another factor that acts as a deterrent and handicap to the Independent is that £100 deposit, frozen until after the election and passing into the Government's maw if a sufficient quota is not obtained. The only excuse given for this relic of the British regime is that it prevents freak candidates: it prevents, however, only those to whom £100 is a definite loss. The wealthy freak is not hampered. There are other ways of eliminating the 'freak', a larger number of nominators, for instance; say one hundred nominations in the area by responsible citizens. But here again the Big Parties do not worry: for them the fewer the candidates the better. That the three Independent women should have had to pay £300 to swell the Government's coffers savours of the cruelty condemned in the Bible of seething the kid in its mother's milk. It punishes the citizen who has the spirit to stand against the Big Battalions.

If women in Ireland are not yet sufficiently educated politically to vote for women the blame rests largely with the various political machines that disregard them save as mere voting conveniences. Certain blame, too, of course, attaches to the women themselves, those smug ones especially, who declare that they have 'no interest in politics.' There are still great possibilities in PR if properly applied. Should the nation's woman-power be mobilized to full strength – as it is in the Soviet Union, for instance – it could be made possible to include women on each panel from each party, so that each elector could be given the opportunity of voting for a woman. (In setting up the National University Senate this principle was adopted to ensure that the Senate would not be entirely male.) A slower process would be the other alternative of peaceful penetration by women into the party-machines, and of educating public opinion by training women to take more than a mere silent part in politics. Yet women and yes-men are in the long-run mere dead weight, though parties like them. (Some one has suggested flippantly that if the statue of Queen Victoria were placed inside the Dáil it might replace inexpensively one of the robots now sitting there.)

The challenge to the party-system has at least been made by the Independent women; their election campaign has set the public thinking. It took a while before the slogans 'Equal Pay' and 'A Square Deal for Women' on Dublin's boardings were superseded by the device of 'Bisurated Magnesia.' When next an election comes the seed sown should be ready to germinate – the seed beneath the snow as Silone calls it, speaking of those seeds of new growths that lie for a while submerged, but living.

Hanna Sheehy-Skeffington: 'Women in Politics',
The Bell, Vol. 7, no. 2, 1943, pp. 143-8

REFERENCES

Details given here consist of books and articles in books and journals.
Reference to articles extracted from newspapers are given in full in the text.

BOOKS

Behan, Brian: *Mother Of All The Behans: the autobiography of Kathleen Behan as told to Brian Behan*, London, Hutchinson, 1984.

Bhuitleir, Máire de: 'When the Sinn Féin Policy was Launched', in (ed.) W G Fitzgerald, *The Voice of Ireland*, Dublin and London, Virtue and Co., n.d. pp. 105-109.

Buckley, Margaret: *A Jangle of the Keys*, Dublin, Duffy, 1938.

Chonail, Eilis Bean Uí: 'A Cumann na mBan Recalls Easter Week', *Capuchin Annual* 1966, pp. 271-8.

Coyle, Eithne: in (ed.) Uinseann MacEoin, *Survivors*, Dublin, Argenta, 1980, pp. 151-60.

Dhonnchadha, Sighle Bean Uí: in (ed.) Uinseann MacEoin, *Survivors*, Dublin, Argenta, 1980, pp. 331-53.

Fitzgerald, William G. (ed.): *The Voice of Ireland*, Dublin and London, Virtue and Co., n.d. (1920s).

Fox, R M: *Louie Bennett, Her Life and Times*, Dublin, Talbot Press, n.d. (1958).

Gavan-Duffy, Louise: 'In Tsan GPO: Cumann na mBan' in (ed.) F X Martin, *1916 and University College Dublin*, Dublin, Duffy, 1967, pp. 91-5.

Gifford Czira, Sydney: *The Years Flew By*, Dublin, Gifford and Craven, 1974.

Gonne MacBride, Maud: *A Servant of the Queen*, London, Victor Gollancz, 1974 (first published 1938).

Litton, Helen (ed.): *Revolutionary Woman: Kathleen Clarke,* Dublin, O'Brien Press, 1991.

Mac Eoin, Uinseann: *Survivors*, Dublin, Argenta, 1980.

Macken, Mary: 'W B Yeats, John O'Leary and the Contemporary Club', in *Studies (Ireland),* Vol. xxviii, 1939, pp.136-42.

Markievicz, Constance de: *Prison Letters*, London, Virago, 1987 (first published 1934).

Martin, F.X. (ed.): *The Howth Gun-Running*, Dublin, Browne and Nolan, 1964.

Martin, F X (ed.): *1916 and University College Dublin*, Dublin, Duffy, 1967.

McKenna, Kathleen: 'The Irish Bulletin', *Capuchin Annual* 1970, pp. 503-27.

O'Brien, Nora Connolly: in (ed.) Uinseann Mac Eoin, *Survivors*, Dublin, 1980, pp. 183-215.

O'Callaghan, Mrs K: 'A Curfew Night in Limerick', in (ed.) W G Fitzgerald, *The Voice of Ireland*, Dublin and London, Virtue and Co., n.d. pp. 147-50.

Sheehy-Skeffington, Hanna: *Impressions of Sinn Féin in America*, Dublin, Davis Publishing Co., 1919.

Shiubhlaigh, Máire Nic: *The Splendid Years*, Dublin, Duffy, 1955.

Skinnider, Margaret: *Doing My Bit for Ireland*, New York, Century, 1917.

Smithson, A M P: *In Times of Peril: Leaves From the Diary of Nurse Linda*

   Kearns, *from Easter Week 1916 to Mountjoy 1921*, Dublin, Talbot Press, 1922.

Smithson, Annie M.P.: *Myself – and Others*, Dublin, Talbot Press, 1944.

Spring Rice, Mary: 'Diary of the *Asgard*', in (ed.) F X Martin, *The Howth Gun-Running*, Dublin, Browne and Nolan, 1964, pp. 68-97.

Wyse-Power, Senator Mrs J: 'The Political Influence of Women in Modern Ireland', in (ed.) W G Fitzgerald, *The Voice of Ireland*, Virtue and Co., n.d. pp. 158-61.

Young, Ella: *Flowering Dusk*, London, Dobson, 1945.

UNPUBLISHED MANUSCRIPTS
Máire Comerford: *Autobiography*.
Helga Woggon: *Winnie Carney, A Silent Radical*, Berlin, 1983.
Helena Moloney: *The Citizen Army and the Easter Rising*, radio interview.

JOURNALS
An Phoblacht 1925-1937
Bean na h-Éireann 1908-1911
Capuchin Annual, 1966, 1970
Eire 1923-1924
Irish Bulletin 1919-1921
Irish Citizen 1912-1920
Irish Freedom 1910-1914
Irish Freedom 1926-1937
Irish Volunteer 1914-1916
Leader 1909
Liberty, journal of the Irish Transport and Worker's Union, March-October 1966.
Prison Bars 1937-1938
Republican Congress 1934-1935
Shan Van Vocht 1896-1899
United Irishman 1899-1906

NATIONAL LIBRARY OF IRELAND
Czira Papers.
Eva Gore-Booth Papers.
Sheehy-Skeffington Papers.

Articles by Constance de Markievicz:
Women, Ideals and the Nation, 1909.
What Irish Republicans Stand For, 1923.

Cumann na mBan Convention Reports: 1917, 1918, 1921, 1924, 1933.
Cumann na mBan Executive: 'The Present Duty of Irishwomen', n.d. (1918).
Cumann na mBan Journal, 1926.
Cumann na mBan: 'Ghosts', n.d. (1929).

Sinn Féin Convention Report, 1917.
Sinn Féin: Appeal to the Women of Ireland, 1918.

Sinn Féin Publicity Department: Press statements, 1922.

Women's Social and Progressive League: Open Letter to Women Voters, n.d. (1938).

Mná na hEireann: 'Mná na hEireann', leaflet, 1933.

Dáil Eireann: Official Report: Debate on the Treaty Between Great Britain and Ireland signed in London on 6th December, 1921, Dublin, Stationery Office, n.d.
Private Sessions of Second Dáil, Dublin, n.d.

American Commission on Conditions in Ireland, Interim Report, 'Memorandum on British Atrocities in Ireland 1916-20', Washington, n.d. (1921).

NEW YORK PUBLIC LIBRARY
John Quinn Papers: Berg Collection.

FURTHER READING:
The following books provide useful accounts of women's involvement in nationalist, suffrage and labour organisations. More detailed bibliographies can be found in Hill and Pollock: *Image and Experience* and in Luddy and Murphy: *Women Surviving*.

Coulter, Carol: *The Hidden Tradition: Feminism, Women and Nationalism*, Cork University Press, 1993.
Cullen Owens, Rosemary: *Smashing Times, A History of the Irish Women's Suffrage Movement 1889-1922*, Dublin, Attic Press, 1984.
Cullen Owens, Rosemary: *Did Your Granny Have a Hammer?* Dublin, Attic Press, 1985. (Collection of facsimile documents.)
Curtis, Liz: *The Cause of Ireland: From the United Irishmen to Partition*, Belfast, Beyond the Pale, 1994.
Gallagher, S.F. (ed.): *Women in Irish Legend, Life and Literature*, Gerrards Cross, Colin Smythe, 1983.
Haverty, Anne: *Constance Markievicz*, London, Pandora, 1988.
Hill, Myrtle and Pollock, Vivienne: *Image and Experience: Photographs of Irishwomen 1880-1920*, Belfast, Blackstaff Press, 1993.
Holmes, Janice and Urquhart, Diane: *Coming into the Light: The Work, Politics and Religion of Women in Ulster 1840-1940*, Belfast, the Institute of Irish Studies, Queen's University, 1994.
Innes, C.L.: *Woman and Nation in Irish Literature and Society 1880-1935*, London, Harvester, 1993.
Jones, Mary: *These Obstreperous Lassies, A History of the Irish Women Workers Union*, Dublin, Gill and MacMillan, 1988.
Lawrenson Swanton, Daisy: *Emerging from the Shadow*, Dublin, Attic Press, 1994.
Levenson, Leah and Natterstad, Jerry: *Hanna Sheehy-Skeffington, Irish*

Feminist, Syracuse University Press, 1986.

Loftus, Belinda: *Mirrors: William III and Mother Ireland*, Dundrum, Picture Press, 1990.

Luddy, Maria and Murphy, Cliona (eds.): *Women Surviving: Studies in Irish Women's History in the 19th and 20th Centuries*, Dublin, Poolbeg, 1989.

MacBride, Maud Gonne: *The Gonne-Yeats Letters, 1893-1938*, (eds.) Anna MacBride White and A. Norman Jeffares, London, Hutchinson, 1992.

MacCurtain, Margaret and Ó Corrain, Donncha (eds.): *Women in Irish Society: The Historical Dimension*, Dublin, Arlen House, 1978.

MacLochlainn, Alf and Sheehy-Skeffington, Andree: *Writers, raconteurs and notable feminists*, Dublin, National Library of Ireland Society, 1993.

Mulvihill, Margaret: *Charlotte Despard*, London, Pandora, 1989.

Murphy, Cliona: *The Women's Suffrage Movement and Irish Society in the Early Twentieth Century*, London, Harvester, 1989.

Norman, Diana: *Terrible Beauty: A Life of Constance Markievicz*, London, Hodder & Stoughton, 1987.

O'Neill, Máire: *From Parnell to De Valera: a biography of Jennie Wyse-Power*, Dublin, Blackwater Press, 1991.

Sawyer, Roger: *'We are but Women': Women in Ireland's History*, London, Routledge, 1993.

Smythe, Ailbhe (ed.): *A Dozen Lips*, Dublin, Attic Press, 1994.

Ward, Margaret: *Unmanageable Revolutionaries: Women and Irish Nationalism*, London, Pluto, 1983.

Ward, Margaret: *Maud Gonne: A Life*, London, Pandora Press, 1990.

SMASHING TIMES

A history of the Irish women's suffrage movement, 1889-1922

Rosemary Cullen Owens

While Irish nationalists were battling for Home Rule and the affairs of the Land League, Irish women were also battling for the basic right to vote.

Smashing Times brings to life the Irish women of the 1900s who were active and militant suffragists. It is a unique and enthralling account of how they fought for women's rights, particularly the right to vote, how they set about obtaining their objectives, how they were viewed by the Irish public, priests and politicians. It also examines their historic achievement and their effect on Irish society.

'Rosemary Cullen Owens has written the engrossing story of how Irish women broke through massive obstacles and achieved the vote by 1928' *Margaret MacCurtain*

£8.99

FROM DUBLIN TO NEW ORLEANS

The journey of Nora and Alice

Suellen Hoy and Margaret MacCurtain

In the autumn of 1889, Nora and Alice, two young twenty-year-old women, left the relative security of their Dominican convent boarding school at Cabra in north Dublin. They set off on a journey so far removed from their daily lives that the resulting diaries recording their adventures make engrossing reading.

The purpose of their journey was not to make their fortune but to begin a life in religion as Dominican sistersin New Orleans.

'Whether or not you were a Dominican pupil like me, you will find the story riveting' *Patricia Scanlan*

£9.99

A LINK IN THE CHAIN

The story of the Irish Housewives Association 1942-1992

Hilda Tweedy

'During a campaign that demanded school meals for children, one reverend gentleman said that the Irish Housewives Association would be breaking up the sanctity of the home if children were to be fed at school.'

in 1942, during the 'Emergency', a group of women met to discuss the dreadful conditions in which some women and children were living. These women founded the Irish Housewives Association, an immensely influential pressure group which was to go on speaking out about injustices and the needs of Irish women, inside and outside the home, for the next fifty years.

Founder member Hilda Tweedy recalls issues as diverse as employment equality and Buy Irish campaigns in a history of a movement that has touched the lives of all Irish women over the last half century.

£5.99

EMERGING FROM THE SHADOW

The lives of Sarah Anne Lawrenson and Lucy Olive Kingston

Daisy Lawrenson Swanton

Emerging from the Shadow is the story of two generations of women. The diaries of Sarah Lawrenson and her daughter Lucy Kingston give a wonderfully atmospheric picture of life in Wicklow and Dublin - from Dalkey to Rathmines - in the late nineteenth century.

Sarah Lawrenson courageously supported herself and her husband after her husband died, leaving her with four small children; Lucy Kingston campaigned for the rights of women and for peace. She became involved in the suffrage movement, the Women's International League for Peace and Freedom, and CND. Her story is full of personal social detail and political history.

£10.99